Establishing interdisciplinary programs in the middle school

Establishing interdisciplinary programs in the middle school

Philip Pumerantz

Ralph W. Galano

Parker Publishing Company, Inc.   West Nyack, N.Y.

Library of Congress Cataloging in Publication Data

Pumerantz, Philip.
   Establishing interdisciplinary programs in the
middle school.

   Includes bibliographical references.
   1. Junior high schools. 2. Project method in
teaching. 3. Group work in education. I. Galano,
Ralph W., 1931-   joint author. II. Title.
LB1623.P84   373.1'3   72-3221
ISBN 0-13-289231-6

Printed in the United States of America

The case for an interdisciplinary approach

Consider a hypothetical interdisciplinary classroom situation in a typical middle school: Our attention focuses upon some activity generated by a group of students who are obviously involved with their teacher. The teacher appears to be leading a discussion in an area of the language arts. The material in use seems to indicate that the students are analyzing an example of poetry. However, is it poetry? We soon learn that the teacher is not an English teacher, but is a music teacher who is making a point common to both arts and, for the time being, is more easily expressed through poetry.

At the same time, and in another setting, the English teacher may be lending some new insights to another discipline. Both teachers have moved beyond the superficial level of subject-matter "correlation," and have become participants in each other's disciplines. They have employed the interdisciplinary approach. In so doing, their pupils have found an increased relevance in both music and language arts. These pupils, like their predecessors, could have been led to believe that knowl-

7

edge is compartmentalized into various slots, each separate, fragmented and totally unrelated to each other. Victims of the lecture-regurgitation method might have been denied the opportunity of experiencing the meaningful interrelationships existing between science, math, English, the arts or the social sciences. However, these students have participated in an exciting experience which can result from the interdisciplinary approach.

In conventional practice, school subjects are frequently taught as if they were completely unrelated to each other and as if the principal purpose of learning was to pass examinations in specific subjects. Many lose sight of the common ground existing between various disciplines and fear the loss of the uniqueness of their subject and its place in the curriculum. They fail to admit that sometimes some concepts can be imparted better through subjects other than theirs. Instead, teachers should seek to acquaint students with the creations of their contemporaries and predecessors, and to interrelate areas of knowledge to form a comprehensive understanding of themselves. An interdisciplinary approach, then, recognizes the uniqueness of areas of knowledge and disciplines, while at the same time it seeks to observe the interrelationships between them. It views them as a whole or, in the least, as natural allies.

In a practical sense, the interdisciplinary approach is a way of organizing a school in terms of curriculum, instruction, and staffing. Significantly, it can enhance and stimulate the development of innovative arrangements in a school program. As a consequence, it is compatible with team-teaching, individualization of learning, prescriptive learning, nongradedness, flexible schedules, core programs, etc.

Consider a few instructional possibilities for middle school children which can provide many opportunities for activities which enable the child to proceed from areas of strength as well as interest and then be viewed positively by himself and by his peers. For example, while dealing with a topic like America's Period of Westward Expansion, the teacher may recognize a child's interest in folk music, and may allow him to pursue part of this topic through this medium. He might be encouraged to do appropriate research, learn specific ballads, and generally become the "authority" in this area. He can ultimately share his materials with classmates.

In other cases, groups of children can become immersed in an artistic process, and begin to ask the same questions that the artist did, or, likewise, the scientist or the mathematician. The teacher can introduce a concept or discuss an historical epoch, then divide the group into subgroups, and assign individual responsibility for becoming "expert" in a particular phase of the overall concept. The child may develop this individually, with the original teacher, or with the help of another member of the teaching team. The final result will be the pulling together of all the information gathered in this experience of discovery and involvement.

Conversely, the student might approach this technique from an area of weakness. The teacher might identify an area needing support, and then structure the program accordingly. What is most important here is the fact that the teacher will have more opportunity to build an appropriate course of action, often in concert with his colleagues.

The advantages of the interdisciplinary approach for pupils in the middle school may be summarized as follows: It allows pupils —

1. To develop better understandings of themselves and to work out areas of weakness without harm to their self-images;
2. To proceed at a pace commensurate with their interests, skills, and experiences;
3. To have more opportunity to reinforce and improve skills, pursue special interests or details, or to experience inquiry processes;
4. To see present interrelationships and focus upon past and present cultures; and
5. To have experience in developing their individual responsibilities.

Moreover, from the perspective of the staff and the program, this approach provides for —

1. Multiple instructional groups and independent study which help teachers focus on the individual;
2. Better communication among teachers and among students, and between teachers and students;
3. More effective use of innovations in instructional media and technology;

4. Development of independent study which can provide re-
   treats from the competitive activity which is often excessive
   in our school society;
5. Better utilization of staff talents, interests and expertise;
   and
6. More effective use of team-teaching and large- and small-
   group instruction to the end that these can release some
   staff for more preparations and research or to work with
   cluster groups or individuals.

Through interdisciplinary programs, moreover, teachers can develop positive situations for creative teaching. The program can
have the aspect of the open door and not be burdened by matters extraneous to learning, such as rigid time allotments, teacher
domination, one textbook, and indifferent attention to what is
truly primary and what is truly secondary. The necessary involvement of the teacher is commensurate with that of the student, with the consequence that both will work harder in the
process. For example, at a strategic point, the teacher may become less concerned with materials, and shift from one area to
another, and follow a valid tangent on which the students may
lead him. He must know when students have something important to contribute, and be willing to take an occasional back-
seat.

The freedom and flexibility which can exist in the middle
school makes interdisciplinary programming feasible and practical and indeed educationally sound. It can be introduced in
traditional settings and can initially involve a small portion of
the staff and student body. In any case, it can be introduced
within present budgetary and administrative frameworks, and
requires only imagination, enthusiasm, and commitment on the
part of teachers and administrators.

In the following chapters, practical and workable organizational and instructional possibilities will be given for building
interdisciplinary programs in the middle school.

Philip Pumerantz
Ralph W. Galano

Contents

two

The level II, or seventh and eighth programs   37

Restructuring the curriculum
Developing units and materials
Interdisciplinary models
Ungrading the program
Making use of community resources to provide
    more relevant experiences

three

Determining the most effective use of the plant   53

Designing a new plant
Developing individualized learning environments in existing schools

four

How to interest and involve the staff   74

Inservice education: the professional development responsibility
Inservice strategies and vehicles
Some professional development models

five

How to schedule interdisciplinary programs   92

Planning time for the staff
Flexibility in structure
Staff, space utilization
Individualizing instruction
Remedial-enrichment groups
Independent study and contracts

appendix iii

Establishing interdisciplinary programs in the middle school

one

Building realistic
interdisciplinary programs
for grade six, or level I

In this, and the following chapter, we will develop interdisciplinary programs and models, based upon division of the
curriculum into three general components.

1. The Humanities area
2. The Sequential area
3. The Personal Development area.

This reflects a departure from the traditional curriculum design, which identifies both "academic and special subjects,"
and is consistent with current thinking in the middle school
movement. For example, Alexander designates the middle school
curriculum in similar terms, and suggests that activities fall into
three areas also.[1]

---

[1]William M. Alexander and faculty-student seminars. Mimeographed material
from Middle School Institute, University of Florida, College of Education, Summer, 1966-67.

Learning Skills Areas

Continuation and expansion of basic communicational and computational skills development begun at the primary school level. Remedial programs of skills development.

General Studies Area

Areas giving the learner an awareness of his cultural heritage and other common learnings essential to civic and economic literacy. Content involves major concepts and themes drawn from the disciplines of literature, social studies, math, science and fine arts. It is in this general area that much of our interdisciplinary activity will take place.

Personal Development Area

Personal and remedial needs. Exploration of personal interests growth, technical training, student-managed enterprises and work projects.

During the course of this chapter we will discuss more flexible approaches to grouping. It is not necessary at this point to digress into the various pros and cons regarding homogeneous, heterogeneous or variable pupil grouping. We will propose, however, that the interdisciplinary approach will have applications for all three grouping methods. In fact, the rationale of this book is based upon the assumption that interdisciplinary programs can readily become effective in the majority of our "typical" school programs. The attempt is more practical than philosophical for we subscribe to the position held by Howard and Bardwell:

> Unsuccessful attempts to produce an enduring design litter the path of educational history. It may be that the problem is insoluble. Nevertheless we must persevere so that eventually there may be at least one close approximation to success in our repertoire of educational techniques.[2]

---

[2]E. R. Howard and R. W. Bardwell, *How to Organize a Non-Graded School* (Englewood Cliffs, N.J.: Prentice-Hall, 1966) p. 3.

HOW TO DESIGN INTERDISCIPLINARY
STRATEGIES FOR TEACHING

In his "repertoire" of classroom experiences, the creative teacher can find, literally, hundreds of instances where inter-relationships between subjects can enrich the learning experience. For example, there are numerous instances where he might use an art form to illustrate a scientific principle, or to clarify a difficult structural principle in grammar. Good teachers do this often in the normal course of their teaching. This chapter will focus on two discussions: (1) a consideration of the type of *strategy* described above, with some examples of typical areas of interrelationship involving the individual teacher, and (2) the elaboration of a formal team-approach which might be incorporated into the level I design. This will involve an exploration of the humanities approach, with its organizing principles and philosophical basis.

To start, let us consider a few of the potential interdisciplinary possibilities which can confront the individual 6th grade teacher in every school.

The 6th grade curriculum, for example, often involves the Old World. A unit on Ancient Greece might involve her chronological place in history, or a study of those political factors which provided the basis for later Western political and cultural institutions. But how often do we seize upon the other possibilities which may provide more relevance to this topic, and to a broader experience for the student? For instance, Pythagoras is usually mentioned in very general terms during this period, usually being associated with certain mathematical principles. A little research will reveal his contributions toward the basis of Western music. His studies into the nature of scale modes involve an important reference to the cultural context of the music of his day. However, a more important implication of his work is found in the acoustical principles which emerged from his musical activities, and are important to our physical sciences. We can pursue this further, but the significant point is that the wise teacher will encourage the development of an otherwise limited or irrelevant idea into areas which can generate a valid and meaningful involvement on the part of the student. This can be a process of enriching the lesson by example, or more effectively, can be the basis for independent study on the part of individual students. The mere memorization of the fact that Pythagoras was a Greek scholar and scientist is not nearly as significant as the process of learning that the above activity can generate

In another school it might be more appropriate to use Western culture as a point of departure for an investigation of Afro-Asian culture. Either by comparison or by contrast, the teacher might use art forms, folk forms, language, historical factors and may proceed to the familiar to the more complex, both in the classroom and in the independent study experience. The possibilities are numerous, and a kind of "domino theory" of learning seems to emerge when individual students are given the opportunity to explore areas associated with a central theme. Each step seems to lead to another, opening doors to and through other disciplines. The following illustration shows a more structural implication of interrelationships between disciplines:

INTERRELATING THE AREAS OF LANGUAGE ARTS WITH MUSIC AND ART WHEN STUDYING THE PARAGRAPH IN ENGLISH

A discussion of the paragraph will involve

1. Paragraph sense
2. Developing a topic
3. Unity and coherence
4. Transition and connectives
5. Stylistic examples.

Musical examples which might be referred to through musical literature could provide an aural and visual experience with:

1. Form and structure, i.e., ABA forms
2. Use of thematic material
3. Rhythmic structures and repeated phrases. Transactions
4. Harmonic structures
5. Polyphony or monoph ony
6. Styles.

Art examples can provide visual experiences including:

1. Composition, form
2. Structure, perspective
3. Color, shading
4. Thematic function
5. Styles.

As an example of a possible interdisciplinary program for grade 6 in the middle school, study the following student program guide to see how music is interrelated with art, English, social studies, and science.

INDIVIDUAL AND GROUP PROJECTS

GROUP I

Complete number 1, and any others assigned.

1. With your music teacher's approval, choose any one of the following subjects as it relates to ancient or medieval history. Gather as much information as possible, becoming your class's "authority" in this field. When we have further discussions concerning the music of these periods, your teacher should feel free to call upon you if he feels that he can relate music material to your subject. He will assist you in determining the type of material you should look for. In certain cases, two or more students may work together.

Interest Areas		
Drama	Science and Dis-	Education
Dance	covery	Trade or Com-
Poetry	Olympic Games	merce
Literature	Painting	Guilds
Religion	Sculpture	Tournaments
Warfare	Architecture	Crusades

2. Draw or build a model of one of the Ancient or Medieval instruments mentioned in the text. It must be an accurate drawing, or a full size or scale model of wood, clay or other appropriate medium. Be prepared to explain the following:

a. How it worked. Describe such things as the resonator, tuning devices, and how pitches were changed upon it.

b. Mention instruments which developed from it.

(You may want to use art or shop facilities for this project. Arrangements then must be made with all teachers involved.)

3. Sparta and Athens were two of the Greek City-States. Compose an essay discussing the following:

   a. Music was important to both Spartans and Athenians, but it flourished in Athens. Why?

   b. The Spartans used music for purposes different than the Athenians. What do you think they were? Why?

4. Make an illuminated manuscript no smaller than 8½ x 11 inches. Details to be explained.

5. Compose the text of a ballad. Details to be explained, after completion of discussion of ballads.

6. Listed below are vocabulary words having the same root as words in the text. Find the corresponding word in the text. For example:

   Chorous - Chorus
   School   - Schola

   Rite
   Tubular
   Acoustical
   Ethics
   Gymnasium
   Canticle
   Gregorian Calendar
   Dominate
   Unit
   Congregate
   Monastic
   Gallic
   Polyunsaturated
   Fiddle

7. Make a crossword puzzle using at least 15 vocabulary words from the text (use the capitalized words).

8. Listed below are the periods of music history. We have discussed the first two and should become familiar with the others. *Dates* are approximate.

Ancient	— 2500 B.C. to 200 A.D.
Medieval	— 200 A.D. to 1450
Renaissance	— 1450 to 1600
Baroque	— 1600 to 1750
Classical	— 1750 to 1820
Romantic	— 1820 to 1900

Post Romantic and Modern after 1900

List five important events occurring during each period (not musical events).

GROUP II

1. Locate in the Bible some of the places where music is mentioned. List examples in detail.

2. Prepare a chart, diorama, time-line, or drawing which represents interesting information about ancient or medieval music. Details must be accurate.

3. Locate an example of art, sculpture, literature, drama, dance, or architecture of either period. Can it be compared with the music of that time?

4. Describe a Greek play and discuss the ways music was used in comedies or tragedies.

5. Complete a short essay on one of the following topics:

Music in the Life of Primitive Man
Ancient Musical Instruments
Medieval Musical Instruments
Music of the Hebrews
Music in Education (Greek or Medieval)
Famous Musicians of the Middle Ages
Famous Minstrels or Troubadours
Musical Contributions of the Christian Monks
Music in the Monastery
Music in the Medieval Castle
Famous Songs of the Minstrels
Musical Notation
Part Music
Gregorian Chant
Music of the Crusades
Byzantine Music

6. Learn an example of either medieval ballad, Hebrew, or Gregorian Chants. Sing it for your class. This may require the assistance of your music teacher.

7. There were many secular dances developed during the Middle Ages. Some survived until many years later — describe some of them. It might be possible to perform one of them with the assistance of a few of your classmates.

8. Make a bibliography of ten books available in the School Library. Include those which would be of interest to *sixth graders* studying the materials in the text. This may include any subject area.[3]

Possible interrelation combinations. A brief list of interrelated studies for level I, which may be successful in the middle schools, is offered below:[4]

1. *Social studies and math* — Trace the history of the Hindu Arabic numeration system in social studies. How did practical geometry emerge in the Middle East?

2. *Social studies and science* — The social studies will involve climate, topographic features, maps, and the study of earth science will involve an appropriate reciprocation toward the social studies. It can also involve the emergence of scientific thought as opposed to superstition, scientific principles espoused by Archimedes, Euclid, Socrates, and Aristotle.

3. *English, science and math* — The English program will involve men of math and science during class readings or individual reports.

4. *English and social studies* — This will involve an interchange of literature with the social or political trends of a period being covered in social studies, for example, Colonization-Evangeline.

5. *Social studies and libraries* — Beginnings of libraries in Ancient Greece, Egypt and Rome. The "library" functions of Medieval scholars and monks.

---

[3]R. W. Galano, *Music Foundations.* Grade 6, A School Improvement Fellowship, Public Schools, Scarsdale, N.Y., Summer, 1965.

[4]Suggested by mimeographed middle school Curriculum Guide dated 8/68, Public Schools, Pleasantville, N.Y., p. 62.

6. *Science and math* — The practical applications in science of the metric system.

7. *Social studies and industrial arts* — This will involve drawing and planning activities related in project construction for industrial arts.

8. *Social studies and English* — This can involve integration of myths and legends, traced from ancient civilizations to the minstrels and bards of the Middle Ages.

9. *Science, math and art* — This could entail the use of mechanical drawing or use of numerical scales.

10. *Music and art* — By their comprehensive nature they can be related to all areas, pulling ideas together or providing more tangible examples of certain principles.

This is only a partial list. Other possibilities will depend upon the creativity of the teacher, and, in many cases, of the student.

Figure 1-1 illustrates what student schedules might look like when based upon a more traditional time sequence. Note the rotation of special class areas between two 6th grade classes and the possibilities for interrelation combinations.

HOW TO DEVELOP INTERDISCIPLINARY TECHNIQUES ENCOMPASSING TEAM-TEACHING

We will now consider a more formal application of the interdisciplinary idea which takes advantage of curricular and instructional practices complementary to this type of approach. Some of these practices are as follows:

1. Team-teaching
   Subject-matter specialists combined in an interdisciplinary team.
2. Variable grouping
3. Modular and core scheduling
4. Independent study
5. Large-group instruction
6. Small-group instruction
7. Use of learning centers.

Figure 1-1

Combined Interdisciplinary-Traditional Schedule
for a Sixth Grade Student

Schedule

Time	Monday	Tuesday	Wednesday	Thursday	Friday
8:00 10:00	INTERDISCIPLINARY BLOCK Language Arts Social Studies Science				
10:00 10:50	Foreign Language	Music	Foreign Language	Art	Independent Study (Open-School)
10:50 12:00	Physical Education	Independent Study (Skills Development)	Physical Education	Foreign Language - - - - - - - Independent Study	Physical Education
12:00 12:30	LUNCH				
12:30 1:30	INTERDISCIPLINARY BLOCK Math				UNIFIED ARTS
1:30	Art	Foreign Language	Personal Development (Group Guidance)	Music	

Interdisciplinary team-teaching in grade 6. A more formal interdisciplinary approach to consider for Level I is the interdisciplinary team design. The humanities approach is the simplest and most effective way of incorporating interdisciplinary teaching into the 6th grade program. It is specific to the general studies area mentioned earlier in this chapter and is involved in an awareness of our culture, past and contemporary, and of man and his relation to both his universe and to himself. It begins with a concern for the human being and of his role in society. Consider the possibilities we have for enriching the learning experience of children. For example, we may investigate, within a sixth grader's context, such exciting areas as:

1. Man and his concern about his environment
2. His relationship with his neighbors
3. His belief in God
4. His quest for beauty, and for a better life
5. His desire for freedom and equality
6. His search for knowledge and truth
7. His relationship to a changing society
8. His concern about his future, and his relationship to the past
9. His use of leisure time.

These are not farfetched concepts which are unrealistically complex for Level I. They can be incorporated into our teaching or, better, can form the fiber of a total conceptual scheme. There are in our schools many teachers who would find it exciting to incorporate these broad ideas, and to encourage children to begin to think in terms of them. There are teachers who are sensitive to the necessity of thinking in terms of more liberal contemplation and an enthusiastic pursuit of ideals.

The vehicles for this are those disciplines which characterize man and his achievements. His literature, art, historical periods, past, achievements, frailties, creations and aspirations are much in evidence in each of the "subjects" already in our curriculum. Through them we see men capable of love, hate, anger and fear, and then proceed to learn how these were manifested by artists, explorers, soldiers and others.

The 6th grade core subjects lend themselves to the humanities approach. Subjects specific to consideration of the ideas enumerated above are English, social studies, reading, music and the arts. It is practical to schedule all of these in one consolidated humanities block, extending into each other whenever desirable. While science and math have much bearing upon this entire scheme, it is appropriate to schedule them in a parallel but associated block. Math, science, and foreign language are the most sequential of the disciplines. The humanities block makes it possible for one discipline to continue where another leaves off, or to support another at a strategic time. Figure 1-2 illustrates the practical application of this in both a modular or common period schedule

Figure 1-2

Possible Schedule — Sixth Graders

18-Minute Modules

Module	Monday	Tuesday	Wednesday	Thursday	Friday
1 2 3 4 5	INTERDISCIPLINARY BLOCK (HUMANITIES) Language Arts Social Studies				
6 7	Music	Art	Music	Art	Independent Study Reading Skills Development Group Guidance
--- 8 ---					
9 10	SEQUENTIAL BLOCK Math				
-- 11 ---					
12	LUNCH				
13 14 15 16 17	SEQUENTIAL BLOCK Science Foreign Language				
18 19 20	Physical Education	Shop Home Economics	Physical Education	Shop Home Economics	Physical Education

The program of activities outlined here shows the types of possibilities in terms of curriculum organization and instruction available for grade 6 using an interdisciplinary approach.

A. *Flexible block period* — The team and classes meet five days weekly, preferably in a room or rooms which are adaptable to large-group instruction.
   1. This flexible period is to be used for both teaching and personal enrichment.
      a. Teachers may work with small groups or individual students and can encourage advanced work or remedial activities.
   2. The weekly program plan or overview will be distributed to students to encourage planning and personal preparation.
B. *Large-group instruction* — This will be available for all students and will involve only those who will benefit from it. Other students may be assigned to other independent activities. Some members of the team may be better skilled in this type of activity, while others may be assigned to smaller groups. Appropriate planning must precede large-group presentations.
C. *Small groups* — These may work alone or with a teacher in areas which involve
   1. Visual aids
   2. Tapes
   3. Discussion
   4. Reading or research groups
   5. Committees
   6. Special interest areas
   7. Remedial work
   8. Seminar groups.

Groups may involve up to about twenty students.

D. *Independent study*
   1. Reading materials
   2. Filmstrips
   3. Recordings
   4. TV
   5. Research into special areas

      6. Students will need encouragement and direction from team members.

  E. *Team meetings* — These will occur during school time, in conjunction with the guidance counselor or other specialists. They will involve:

    1. Discussion of large- and small-group activities.
    2. Scheduling tests
    3. Scheduling special activities
    4. Subject or unit correlation
    5. Student evaluations
    6. Grouping
    7. Planning teacher time to allow individual research or planning
    8. Use of auxiliary personnel
      a. Paraprofessionals
      b. Technicians
      c. Guest lecturers[5].

We will later investigate three methods of presentation within the framework of the humanities block, but for now we will suggest from Figure 1-2 that a team-teaching approach is best. Separate departments may incorporate many of the ideas above within the confines of more traditional scheduling. However, the very designation, *interdisciplinary*, implies at least a minimal amount of interrelation between disciplines.

Team-teaching usually involves a minimum of four teachers and resource personnel, who are in charge of approximately 110 students. The team focuses itself upon the pupils, and its members usually include teachers in English, social studies, foreign language, math, and science, with supporting personnel in reading, guidance, and special areas (see Figure 1-3).

Variable pupil grouping is possible within this framework. The pupil-teacher ratio can extend from one-to-one, to one-to-one hundred and ten. Grouping can be a changing and dynamic activity, and the groups are planned to create for each student the best posture for learning. Grouping can be according to readiness, maturity, achievement, skills interest and needs. The team-teacher is in a good position to share his observations with his colleagues and to individualize student programs according

---

[5]Suggested by the Cumberland Valley Schools, Mechanicsburg, Pennsylvania.

to weaknesses or strengths in broad areas, or in specific skills. Modular units or block programming create possibilities for students to spend as much or as little time as needed, in order to perform definite tasks. It creates an improved structure for εrge- or small-group instruction.

Figure 1-3

Interdisciplinary Team Within Grade 6

Grade 6
English
Social Studies
Foreign Language
Math
Science
Reading
Phys. Ed.
Unified Arts
Guidance

Team-planning usually involves a common time each day for program planning and discussion of student problems. It is an opportunity for teachers to form groups of students on the basis of their needs at a given time.

SUGGESTED INTERDISCIPLINARY METHODS

Teachers may develop strategies according to their strengths and share them with the rest of the team. There are three methods or strategies that are characteristic of the interdisciplinary approach. Two of these instructional methods are specific to the humanities block and assume a team-teaching attitude. The third will be applicable to individual teachers enlisting the occasional support of other disciplines. We turn to these approaches now.[6]

---

[6]For additional suggestions: The reader is referred to: *The Humanities*, Bureau of Secondary Curriculum Development, the New York State Education Department, Albany, 1966.

The comparative method. Each of the teacher participants on the team contributes to a flexible structure, and breaks the concept or idea being considered into various units. Social studies might be a central vehicle, for example, and might involve us in an overall period like the Middle Ages. The period becomes the central factor, but the units are considered both separately and in their interrelationships. For example, a consideration of Urban's call to action at Cleremont might stimulate some discussion of other factors critical to the First Crusade. It might develop into a consideration of the Byzantine policies of Urban and then lead into a comparison between the Byzantine and Roman churches. The art or music of this period might lend relevance to what can become the basis for an exciting "immersion" in historical or cultural experiences.

Gregorian chant, Byzantine music, or Moorish and Turkish influences might come into play, and endless possibilities can emerge from the original topic, which is now enhanced by the presence and availability of specialist-teachers.

The children are encouraged to make contributions according to their interests and backgrounds. This involvement can lead to the achievement of what is the primary goal of the comparative method. The pulling together of many separate ideas by the student creates a view to interrelationships, and the effects of one idea upon another.

The correlative method. This is a core-oriented approach, which has as its basis the integration of ideas after considering disciplines separately. The specific nature of the disciplines are important and we become knowledgeable about them. Each subject is taught unto itself, yet it is part of a total conceptual scheme. We gain many ideas from our knowledge about specific things. The conceptual process through which we gained the idea might become more important than the original idea itself.

This requires thoughtful structure and is intent upon considering an idea, and experiencing it through the unique nature of separate disciplines. The idea of brotherhood, for example, might be expressed in literature, art, or any other discipline, each through its unique being. A total concept of brotherhood will emerge from a combination of these different experiences. This approach, subtle as it may appear, has relevance on level I, but would require extreme planning on the part of the staff.

The supportive method. Here one subject is used as a core and other disciplines are used to support or emphasize an idea. This is the most traditional of the methods and is sometimes thought of as team-teaching. It may be described as a more liberal traditional curriculum design, however. A teacher of a neighboring subject might be called in to illustrate a point at a specific time; perhaps as in the case of the English teacher using literature of a period as a means of emphasizing some principle being discussed during the social studies lesson.

In developing a level I interdisciplinary unit using either of the methods discussed above, we offer the following guide:

Unit (U.S.S.R.)

Pertinent disciplines which will be involved in this unit:

Language arts	Science
Social studies	Supporting personnel
Art	Guidance
Music	Reading
Physical Education	

I. Topic (U.S.S.R.)
    Definition of Areas of Emphasis
    1. Geography
    2. History — Political considerations
    3. Survey of appropriate literature
    4. Music — folk and composed
    5. Art — folk and great artists
    6. Physical education — folk dance, ballet
    7. Science — inventors and scientists

II. Role of the Interdisciplinary Team
    A. Define role of specific disciplines
    B. Define common grounds and related areas
    C. Assign teaching responsibilities
       1. Large group — lessons
          a. Define resources
       2. Small group — individual study or skills, assignments of teachers
    D. Time priorities and factors

E. Choice of approaches
   1. Comparative
   2. Supportive
      a) This will not involve interdisciplinary team, but will require correlation with assisting teachers
   3. Correlative
   4. Possible choice of guiding themes
      a) The team may wish to develop an idea similar to the following, using one of the above approaches:
         (1) (Social Studies) "Compare the U.S.S.R. and the United States in such areas as:"
             (a) Music
             (b) Art
             (c) History
             (d) Population
             (e) National purpose
             (f) Geography
             (g) Science
         (2) (Music) "Some people believe that Americans and Russians are very much alike in temperament, and have many similar likes and dislikes. For example, Russian music is more popular in the United States than is any other music, while American composers are favorites in Russia. Determine whether or not this is true in this and in other areas. Why? Your teacher will discuss this with you further."
F. Choice of appropriate materials and media
G. Grouping of children
   1. Assign projects
   2. Assign groups
H. Evaluation
   Interim evaluation of students and evaluations.

FOUR KEYS TO ORGANIZING INSTRUCTION

Interdisciplinary curricula possibilities can be organized along four major areas of emphasis. These are the following:

1. Chronological
2. Philosophical ideas
3. Value orientation
4. Pragmatic

At different times and in different situations, teachers can use combinations of elements from all four. The prevalent method will be determined by the point of view of the teacher and by the needs of the students. It is not necessary to consider each as a separate approach divorced from the rest. However, for the purposes of clarification we shall discuss each separately.

Chronological. This presents ideas or events in chronological order. We see relationships both to the time of creation of an example and as it affects us today. We learn to understand men by those things which they have created, or as a result of their actions.   This is a good approach where the curriculum emphasizes times and places where dominant concepts were important; for example, the Renaissance, the Age of Exploration, the Industrial Revolution, the Machine Age, Feudalism, or the Atomic Age. This approach is appropriate to interdisciplinary instructional practices in the middle school. In this approach we would tend to emphasize that events are more important than facts. Also, our present experience is often a reflection of the past.[7]

Philosophical. We gain ideas from most of our experiences and inquiries. We want to understand the ideas which were at the basis of a work of art or literature. We seek the answers to specific truths through the consideration of ideas. "Who am I?" "Where am I going?" It is obvious that this might be difficult for younger children to achieve literally. However, the overall concept is not and can be incorporated into middle school teaching. There are many process-oriented experiences which can contribute to this type of organization. Sixth graders enjoy opportunities for role-playing, or immersion in activities which recreate a period of history. The practical example included in this chapter provides a model which was used successfully with sixth graders studying Ancient and Medieval Music and Social Studies. Another approach is a guidance-oriented experience, which confronts the student with issues which are of immediate

---

[7] An unpublished manuscript referring to: A.D. Graffe, *Creative Education in the Humanities*, New York: Harper and Brothers, pp. 11-28.

concern to him. He becomes the focus of his own attention. Group guidance activities can center upon such issues as:
Our Responsibilities
1. To ourselves
2. To our family
3. To our school
4. To our friends
5. To our nation and world.

Middle school youngsters can profit from role-playing, small group discussions, and presentations by pupil personnel staff, teachers, members of administration, and visitors.

For a third model see Appendix I.

Value oriented. Here we discuss an idea, then allow the child an opportunity to explore it through individual study. We structure a concept, then allow the acceptance or rejection of it through discussion with other students. We share different points of view, particularly towards contemporary problems. The teacher may act as a guide, and seeks to develop a desire for inquiry. Students become involved in an idea or point of information, and are encouraged to reject or accept it as a result of individual research or group discussions. This can easily be encouraged in our humanities block. The teacher can introduce a unit, divide the class into subgroups and assign each child a responsibility to become involved in a particular phase of an overall concept. The final result will be the pulling together of all ideas, with the possibility of an exciting conclusion. The teacher's primary role is to structure the program and direct individual learning experiences.

Pragmatic. The work of art is representative of the time of its origin. We stress a pragmatic approach in which each child becomes involved in much the same way the painter, musician, writer, or scientist did, and he begins to ask some of the same questions. We understand interrelationships by "doing." The process becomes important, for we become involved in a creative manner. There is opportunity for self-evaluation and this could eliminate evaluation from without.[8] This is the process of actual involvement. Creative writing, music and art are the primary vehicles for this method.

---

[8] Ibid.

two

The level II, or seventh
and eighth programs

The preceding chapter presented guidelines for implementation of interdisciplinary programs within a traditional program. The approaches presented can easily be extrapolated into the 7th and 8th grade curriculum. More major departures from traditional practices will now be explored. The 7th and 8th grade programs will be referred to alternately as separate grade levels or, in other examples, as a nongraded Level II. The latter, of course, views grade 6 as Level I. Suggestions for interdisciplinary programs will range from short units or conceptual schemes to an examination of more lengthy units of study.

What are some of the real questions facing teachers and administrators who are about to venture into departures from tradition? The authors believe that three major possibilities confront us:

1. The restructuring of the curriculum, allowing orderly movement from separate subject disciplines to interrelated general groups; this transition back and forth must maintain the integrity of the disciplines involved.

2. The necessity for the development of new materials and units.
3. The broadening of the learning experience to make better use of community resources.

RESTRUCTURING THE CURRICULUM

In the preceding chapter reference was made to Alexander's description of the curriculum, in terms of three general areas: (1) learning skills, (2) general studies, and (3) personal development. Alexander has, in effect, categorized related areas of study in broader constellations than single disciplines, and has defined some common ground between them. Atkins suggests that one clearly identifiable trend is a restructuring of the curriculum so that its organization emphasizes the importance of both cognitive and affective development.[1] He illustrates that the Boyce Middle School in Upper St. Clair, Pennsylvania, is organized around three components:

> *Analytical* — Math, science, language. Those areas which stress logical, sequential, and cognitive learning experiences (800 minutes per week).
>
> *Expressive Arts* — Including fine and practical arts, creative expression, performing arts, and world cultures, use of creative, divergent mental and emotional development (650 minutes per week).
>
> *Personal Development* — Including physical education, growth and development, and social dynamics; emphasizes understanding of physical and social growth patterns (450 minutes per week).

The curriculum design suggested by the authors is essentially similar in concept, although terminology differs.

Humanities   — English
Social Studies
Science   } Disciplines
(Art – Music)
(Math)
Remedial Needs

---

[1] Neil P. Atkins, A Keynote Address, The Third *Quo Vadis* Conference, University of Bridgeport, October 25, 1969.

Sequential   — Math
                 Foreign Language
                 (Music – Art)
                 Communication Skills,   }   Disciplines
                 Reading
                 Physical Education
                 Remedial Needs
Personal
Development — Exploratory Projects
                 Remedial Needs
                 Community Activity
                 Independent Projects
                 Enrichment Performing Arts
                 Technical Teaching
                 Student-managed Projects

The authors have been careful to focus upon specific disciplines within the broader general areas, for necessity will require that a reasonable portion of 8th grade time be spent within the "subject" area. This is particularly true in view of the fact that 9th grade and subsequent high school programs are subject-centered; i.e., 8th graders beginning high school level algebra must remain within a very specific and well-defined framework within that subject. It will be seen later that a total interdisciplinary commitment is not always as desirable as smaller ventures into short conceptual or problem-centered units. It is wise to return to the discipline to redirect attention to traditional programs and development of basic and generalized skills. Interdisciplinary focus tends to better develop competence in continued learning and generalized skills. Here the tendency is to emphasize broader abstractions in addition to less cognitive and more concrete processes. Chapter V deals specifically with the many possibilities for providing both types of experiences within a workable schedule. The authors subscribe to the position that both experiences are essential for children at this level. While many valid arguments can be found for independent learning, student-centered activities and open-ended experiences, a reasonable time must be devoted to structured, basic learning skills. We are certainly aware that middle school pupils possess many individual basic skills, covering a wide continuum of experience and maturation. We reject the practice of all students reviewing similar skills at the same time whether they need them

or not. However, many teachers have expressed concern over the
reality that many children in grades 6, 7, or 8 cannot function
within largely individualized learning situations and require the
anchor or security of group experiences. Consequently, the authors suggest a balance between sequential, structured programs
and those which focus upon independent learning. Too often the
procedure has been too far in either direction, with some current
feeling that middle school pupils do not truly possess the desire
for independence often attributed to them. We have heard from
middle school youngsters the perception that independent learning often ends up in busy work, or, as one stated, "a good
way for the teacher to get you off of his back!" Others view
student contracts as "rejection by desertion." It appears a sound
approach to present interdisciplinary experiences in short units
of study, running from one to four weeks. This allows both a
"breather" and an opportunity to reinforce the separate disciplines as needed.

DEVELOPING UNITS AND MATERIALS

One of the problems facing teacher teams involved in prepar-
ing units of study is an obvious lack of materials. This has often
had some positive effect insofar as it has created an opportunity
for effective interaction between the teams in the development
of their unit of study. In many cases a refreshing spontaneity
has occurred, with exciting results. On the other hand, the accumulation of outlines, texts, references and the many resources
necessary has often required an unforeseen amount of preparation, with the consequence that many creatively conceived projects have been abandoned or have been ineffective. The authors
have suggested some alternatives for planning time in Chapter
V. They also point out that many school districts are providing
time during summer curriculum development programs which
enable the development of materials for teaching. If units are
conceived for teaching on a two- to four-week basis, a team of
four or five teachers can compile or develop an effective unit in
a relatively short time when allowed to devote full-time energies
to it. Other districts are now devoting half-days during the
school year for the specific purpose of developing materials and

techniques. Teacher inservice programs are discussed in Chapter IV.

Since ungrading is often possible through interdisciplinary action, it is necessary for teachers of different grade levels to provide time for materials development.

Alternately, many existing programs can provide a springboard for departure into other disciplines. One example is *Man a Course of Study*. This program, often taught in grade 6, has been developed by Education Development Center of Cambridge, Massachusetts. This social studies-oriented program is based upon the theories of Jerome S. Bruner. Bruner has developed a theory of instruction which is based upon his studies of learning and instruction.[2] It lends itself to the developmental processes inherent in the interdisciplinary approach.

Man a Course of Study (MACOS) develops the concepts which are enumerated on the title page of *Man: A Course of Study, Talks to Teachers*.

Man: A Course of Study — An Experimental Social Course for Elementary Schools, Peter B. Dow

The Study of Animals, Niko Tinbergen

Innate and Learned Behavior, Irven DeVore

The Concept of Culture, Hans Guggenheim

Man in the Social World

Why Technology in a Study of Man?, Peter B. Dow and Richard S. Rosenbloom

World View

The Netsilik Eskimos, Knud Rasmussen

The Changing Lives of Canada's Eskimos[3]

A review of each of the above by discipline specialists would indicate behavioral goals and activities which can easily become cross-disciplinary. While the concepts are social studies-oriented in the existing MACOS program, it does not require a great deal

---

[2]Readers are referred to Jerome S. Bruner, *Toward a Theory of Instruction* (Cambridge, Mass.: Belknap Press, Harvard University Press, 1967).

[3]*Man: A Course of Study, Talks to Teachers* (Cambridge, Mass.: Education Development Center, 1969); title page. Reprinted with special permission from the Social Studies Curriculum Program of the Education Development Center.

of imagination to develop creative correlations in other disciplines.

Model 7th or 8th grade units will be provided in an outline form, to illustrate a few of the possibilities which can be incorporated into interdisciplinary "problem" or "concept" units.

INTERDISCIPLINARY MODELS

Model I — The "Living Unit": *An Examination of Community Responsibility.* (Grade 8)

This combines language arts, social studies, art and science.

A. *Proposition:* Where is our community going in terms of long-range planning, population growth (building and zoning), protection of natural resources, recreation, public transportation and safety, pollution, public health, industrial development, public housing and welfare, and other areas of public interest.

B. The process of implementation:

1. The discipline specialists involved define the steps and objectives necessary for fulfillment of some solution to the above proposition.

2. They determine the role of each discipline in this process, and state individual and mutual behavioral goals.

3. They develop lessons and arrange appropriate experiences. They also compile appropriate materials, which are either approached in a parallel or convergent manner, as separate or cross-disciplines.

4. They assign students specific responsibilities; for example:

   a. They can involve all students in a social studies program which considers the problems of local government, history of the community, etc.

   b. Students can be assigned specific committee responsibilities, implemented by field trips.

      (1) Interviews with public officials:

         (a) Mayor

         (b) Recreation Commissioner

         (c) Health Officers — Sanitation

         (d) Police

         (e) Planning-Zoning Commissioner

> (f) Hospital Administrator
> (g) Transportation Commissioner
> (h) Welfare Commissioner
> (i) Superintendent of Schools

They might inquire into such areas as programs covering five- or ten-year periods; i.e., "Where are we going as a community?"

> (2) Interviews with other members of the local power structure:
> > (a) The local newspapers. For example, "What is the editorial policy regarding long-range community objectives?"
> > (b) Political groups. For example, "What are the platforms of political parties?"
> > (c) Civic and minority groups.
> > (d) Church organizations.
> > (e) Public utilities, local industries.
> >
> > The direct association of students with members of the community, both in and out of school, has been one of the most exciting developments in contemporary education.

C. The role of each discipline. Some examples are:
  1. Social Studies
     a. Political ramifications
  2. Language Arts
     a. Communicating the experiences observed. Written and oral skills, photography, taped interviews, etc.
  3. Art
     a. Practical and aesthetic planning
  4. Science
     a. Environmental study
     b. Investigation of resources
     c. Observation of local industries, public health services, etc.

Model II – An Example of a Preliminary Outline of a Unit: *The Nature of Change*

This was prepared by a curriculum committee of the Fox Lane Middle School, Bedford, New York (Spring, 1970), and is included to provide an example of an original simple curriculum scheme. This was later developed into a somewhat different unit, which provided interesting inter-

disciplinary experiences in science, math, physical education, foreign language, language arts, unified arts, and
guidance.

The Nature of Change (a partial listing of thoughts on
discipline participation in the unit)

A. Science: Investigate the cyclic nature of change in
in the sciences, e.g., weather; the change
of matter to energy; the conversion of
one form of energy to another; growth as
a form of change

B. Physical Physical development and fitness in the
Education: context of maturation

C. Social
Studies: Case Study of Change

 a. What conditions are necessary in order for change to occur?

 b. Where do new ideas originate?

 c. What is the relationship between new
ideas and change?

 d. Can change be stopped? How?

 e. What are the consequences of too
rapid change? Too slow?

Changing social patterns: family; peers;
world community

Political and social change: American
Revolution; Black revolution

Cultural change: American immigration
and in-migration

Changing interpretations of ideas: The
American Constitution

D. Foreign The growth of language as change; The
Language: relationship of changes in society to
changes in the language;

The appropriateness of change; formal
to idiomatic and informal usage

F. Language Literature: novels and short stories deal-
Arts: ing with changes in adolescents;

Use of mistakes to promote change and
growth in a series of lessons on a topic,
e.g., composition;

Changing language unit;

Drama and role playing

F. Math:	The development of mathematical thought; the importance of topics changing.
G. Unified Arts:	Changing materials; altering; adding; subtracting; juxtaposing.
	Form follows function. As function changes, so do styles, etc., e.g., furniture.

Model III — Developing a Traditional Humanities Approach

It is possible to develop an arts-oriented program which focuses upon man, with attention to his

Art	Dance
Music	Technology
Language	Inventions

This can involve development of separate units of participation which can be organized according to the following approaches:

1. The chronological development of art, music, literature, etc.
2. Styles reflected in the art form.
3. The structure or form reflected in the art form.

We might develop a unit which incorporates all three of the above. A concept like Beauty might involve

   a. A chronological examination of man's perception of beauty as reflected through his architecture, clothing, or language.
   b. An examination of the styles of various artists, musicians, architects, or writers in terms of their expression of beauty.
   c. An examination of how the practical needs of man contributed to beauty and progress, i.e., printing and communication, graphic arts, etc.
4. A physical or personal involvement in the creation of beauty on the part of students, i.e., dance, fine arts, industrial arts. They might perhaps emulate the styles of an artist or chronoligical period.
5. The comparison of the works of the musician, artist or writer, to better understand the interrelationships of the various disciplines.

Model IV — Becoming Involved in the Investigation of
a Concept or Problem. Example: *Man's Ability to Survive*

A. Man and His Natural Environment
   1. How has man adapted to his environment?
      a. Against forces of nature
      b. How has he changed the environment?
         (1) Positively or negatively
B. Man and His Neighbors
   1. Man and his relation to other men
      a. Friend or enemy
   2. Man and his relation to lower animals
      a. Friend or enemy
C. Man as a Creator
   1. Contributions through building, arts, agriculture,
      education, industrialization, communication, etc.
D. Man as a Destroyer or Waster
   1. Destruction of resources, wars, pollution, etc.
E. The Prospects for Survival
   1. Population growth
   2. Political factors
   3. Environmental factors
   4. Natural resources

We could discuss each part in great detail. However, individual students may become involved in any one of the specific areas and can identify the steps necessary for involvement at their level of interest. They might proceed accordingly:

1. State the problem, i.e., "Man as a destroyer or waster."
2. Formulate the objectives of their investigation.
3. Review resources available for implementation.
4. Outline their proposed procedure for conducting their investigation.
5. Proceed under the direction of the teacher, with their responsibilities defined in terms of objectives and time limitations.

Model V — A Guidance Centered Unit (Grade 8): Using
All Disciplines Under the Direction of the
Guidance Counselor. Example: *Educational-Vocational Planning*

A. Academic and Vocational Assessment
 1. Planning Programs for High School
  a. Requirements for college
  b. Requirements for post-high school employment
 2. Assessment
  a. Interest-Preference Testing
  b. Investigating college major groups, occupations, etc.
B. Field Trips
 1. Visit Industries, Craftsmen, etc.
 2. Develop "Tentative" Occupational Interests; Learn Qualifications, etc.
  a. Spend a day or two visiting or working with a practitioner in that field. Report experiences to classmates.
 3. Visit Training Sources, Colleges, etc.
C. Visits From Members of the Community
 1. Informal Talks About Their Occupation and Training
D. Specific Discipline Teachers Could Be in Charge of Major Occupational Areas
 1. For Example, Science Teacher — Technological Fields; Language Arts: Publishing communications, etc.
E. A Major Emphasis Upon the Changing World of Occupations, to Provide a Basis for Realistic and Flexible Long-range Planning

Model VI — A Unit Based Upon the Problems of Race and Poverty (Grade 8)

This is another example of use of existing materials as a basis of departure for group or individual interdisciplinary action. This can involve guidance, language arts, social studies, art and music.

Excellent materials are provided in the following text-book: *The People Make a Nation*, by M. W. Sandler, E. C. Rozwenc, and E. C. Martin; Allyn and Bacon, Boston, 1971.[4]

Chapter VIII, "Race, Poverty and Youth," presents the proposition, *Can this generation build a better America?*

---

[4] From "Contents" of *The People Make a Nation* by Martin W. Sandler, Edwin C. Rozwenc, and Edward C. Martin. Copyright 1971 by Allyn and Bacon, Inc.; reprinted by permission.

and includes articles written by contemporary leaders involved in these issues. The authors are familiar to young people, and the format lends itself to discussion and further research. The chapter includes excellent examples of contemporary art and poetry. There are also many points where music can be integrated.

The chapter deals with such contemporary issues as urban riots, the March on Washington, Black Nationalism, Anti-Separatism, violent revolt, and others. It includes the writings of Martin Luther King, Stokely Carmichael, Roy Innes, Thurgood Marshall, Roy Wilkins, and includes extremist views. One section deals with the Kerner Commission Report. It provides excellent material for providing the basis of interesting activity for both black and white students.

The chapter is further divided into two additional sections, each detailed, namely, *The Problem of Poverty* and *The Problem of Youth.*

Model VII — An Example of an Integrated Lesson Combining the Disciplines of Science and Music (Eighth Grade Science and Music)

Sound:
  I. Definition
   A. Sound Production
    1. Basic principles of sound energy, i.e., condensations and refractions
   B. Sound Waves
    1. Experiments with longitudinal or compressional waves
    2. Use of tuning fork, spring devices, etc.
   C. Sound Travel and Hearing
  II. Characteristics
   A. Use of Musical Instruments and Oscilloscope to Demonstrate
    1. Pitch
    2. Quality
    3. Beats
    4. Resonance (Timbre)
    5. Sympathetic Vibrations
    6. Echoes
  III. Differentiating Between Types of Sound
   A. Noise

    B. Music

    C. Vocal

    D. Electronic Sounds

  IV. The Science of Acoustics (Controlling Sound)

   V. Experiments with Electronic Music, Stereophonic Sound, etc.

  VI. Individual Projects Which Involve Electronic Experimentation, and the Development of Musical Instruments

 VII. Historical Background

    1. Development of musical instruments

    2. The recording industry

    3. Important scientists involved in experimentation and development (i.e., telephone, radio, sonar, aerodynamics, etc.)

VIII. Meeting Individual Needs

    1. Individual projects release both teachers for the purpose of small group or remedial work in understanding of basic concepts or principles related to this unit.

The above models provide a few illustrations of the many possibilities available for teaching. Graded textbooks and curriculum provide the essential basis and material for learning, but must be adapted to the individual needs and pacing possible in conceptual-problem units of study. Scheduling within larger-block units also makes possible opportunities for ungrading in both Humanities and Sequential Areas. (See Chapter V, Table 14.)

UNGRADING THE PROGRAM

The reorganization of disciplines into continuum will provide the structure for ungrading. The scheduling of Humanities Units or sequential programs so that 7th and 8th graders can be available at the same time, creates many possibilities for meeting the specific needs of each pupil. We will find some practical approaches to this in Chapter V. The rationale is based upon the fact that 7th and 8th graders and staff can eliminate grade boundaries if they are both available simultaneously. Inquiry and skill processes in all disciplines can be organized into either units or levels, with students completing each level at their own rate of learning. Consequently, the former 7th grader may move into what had previously been an 8th grade unit. He moves at a time appropriate to his ability, and after he has completed a sequence of processes and goals.

This not only calls for a clear-cut definition of processes, and statements of concept areas, but it will require continuous readjustment and grouping. The organizational structure must be flexible enough to accommodate the changing placement of pupils. Team teaching is essential, along with the probability that class or group sizes will vary. This is relatively easy to implement in the sequential areas, and might first be initiated in the math area. Behavioral phases are well identified into sequential processes. What remains is for us to allow students to move without the restriction of grade level boundaries. If content is organized into specifically identified phases, planned patterns of movement are then possible, for example, sequences which range from mathematical systems at the beginning of grade 7, to statistics at the end of grade 8. The range of experiences can be divided into roughly fourteen or fifteen units.

Flexible group instruction can provide for the teaching of concepts or operations at various times, with some students moving into independent applications of what has been learned. They may at the appropriate time move ahead or, if necessary, return to the "home-base" for reinforcement. Science might likewise be divided into less sequential and more topical units or "levels," and be ungraded accordingly. Foreign Language offers many possibilities for movement through sequences.

MAKING USE OF COMMUNITY RESOURCES TO PROVIDE MORE RELEVANT EXPERIENCES

Among recent developments within secondary schools are:

1. The movement of students out of the school, to make greater use of community resources. Among these are visits to libraries, field studies and research, use of industrial, commercial, or technical facilities, work study programs, work with craftsmen, work in ghettos, or visits to higher educational facilities.

2. Meaningful school experiences for some disadvantaged youth have been structured through "schools without walls" or store-front academies.

3. A willingness on the part of many members of the community to participate in the education of youngsters. They represent diverse talents, vocational backgrounds or economic levels. We see a willingness on the part of the school to accommodate their supplemental skills in the school setting.

4. A concern on the part of our society that we are not training adequate numbers of tradesmen, skilled laborers or craftsmen. A movement away from the notion that college training is the only respectable route to success in our society.

The middle school can address itself to these new directions. The interdisciplinary program can provide many answers to the challenges presented by young people. Some possibilities are:

1. Group guidance activities making possible routine school visits by members of the community who might address themselves to both vocational or educational information giving, or goal orientation. These can be incorporated into social studies areas at appropriate times, or into areas of personal development.

2. A greater partnership with civic, commercial or industrial resources to provide opportunities for students to visit or to make use of facilities which are coordinated with academic activities.

3. Work-study visits of an exploratory nature for students who have neither the desire nor the ability to pursue higher education. Exploratory periods should be brief, and wide-ranging in experience. These could be implemented in cooperation with craft and labor unions or with individual tradesmen and artists.

4. Exploratory programs for all students which allow for personal development in cultural, vocational or social areas.

5. Student participation in active solution to community problems, i.e., tutoring culturally disadvantaged elementary youngsters, clean-up days, work projects such as planting shrubs in public places, or cleaning public waterways, etc.

6. Use of community volunteers to provide additional one-to-one support for students requiring remedial help, beyond that which the school is equipped to provide, i.e., improving reading skills for disadvantaged youngsters who have fallen behind the

regular academic programs but who do not truly qualify as remedial reading students.

7. Teachers from urban middle schools might be employed to provide group tutoring services for disadvantaged youngsters. For example, the White Plains, N. Y. School System has implemented evening "study-halls" in lower income neighborhoods. This provides an evening session for students needing remedial help and assistance with homework or study skills.

8. Highly skilled professional personnel might provide enrichment experiences for youngsters who demonstrate high-level abilities or interests, i.e., an engineer working with advanced math students.

SUMMARY

Some of the practical problems concerning implementation of the 7th and 8th grade programs have been considered. Model units have been provided for the purpose of showing examples of the many possible avenues available to the creative interdisciplinary teacher. The unit or problem approach has been suggested, for it allows for limited, more conservative departures into interdisciplinary activities. Some examples of more long-range commitments were provided, however. Attention was also given to nongradedness, as well as greater use of community resources.

three

Determining the most effective use of the plant

The process of designing a physical environment in the middle school which can facilitate the interdisciplinary programs discussed in Chapters 1 and 2 will be the purpose of the present chapter. Interdisciplinary programs in middle schools suggest altered perceptions of teaching and learning, of ordering curriculum, of scheduling, grouping and management. Indeed the establishment of interdisciplinary programs provides educators with the opportunity to work in the milieu of the future, now. This suggests that the physical environment, and indeed the social and educational, no longer need to conform to formulas of the past. Therefore the planning of facilities must consider current conditions and at the same time represent ways to prepare for the future. That is, the development of educational facilities must accommodate anticipated changes in education in the future. Ultimately what must be achieved is a harmony between the educational environment and the physical or architectural environment.

To the frustration of many forward-looking educators, rigid

attitudes on the part of staffs exist in old as well as new plants. Hopefully, though, the development of an architectural environment which responds to the altered perceptions of education, and one which responds to current social and educational conditions, will be a powerful force in generating the type of creativity and imagination which will be consistent with the interdisciplinary concept.

In this regard, the editors of *The American School Board Journal* have written:

> The design of a new middle school, or the conversion of an existing structure into a middle school facility, permits the development of new physical environments for the teachers and students that can accelerate changes in the ways they behave. How functions within a building are grouped, the use of carpet in a student dining area, or the configuration of group instructional space should play an important role in changing how people act. If change for the better is the name of the game, then the design of the middle school facility becomes a critical element in the success of the middle school concept.[1]

In determining the most effective use of the plant in interdisciplinary programs, two main ideas will be developed, namely, designing a new plant and adapting the existing environment to modern learning conditions. In the latter, attention will focus on guidelines for developing tomorrow's schools with yesterday's facilities, while the former will focus on designing a new middle school plant to accommodate an interdisciplinary program. In both instances, however, the concept of the open learning environment will be featured.

DESIGNING A NEW PLANT

The open environment for learning. A physical plant for a middle school which hopes to incorporate interdisciplinary programs, team teaching and preparation, learning center units, large and readily available learning and resource centers, flexible schedules, and one which focuses on the individualization of the

---

[1]The Editors, "28 Ways to Build Mistakes Out of Your Middle School," *The American School Board Journal* (July, 1970), 17-24.

instructional process calls for educational space which is a far cry from the traditional "eggcrate" school building. The typical "eggcrate" physical plant has several distinct characteristics which place limitations upon instructional program flexibility and hinder implementation of an open environment. For example, the standard classroom unit, 750-900 square feet, tends to dictate groupings of students in clusters of 25-30 for a fixed period of instructional time predetermined by scheduling needs, administrative convenience or some other noninstructional rationale. The standard physical plant with its identical sized classrooms along a double loaded corridor makes it difficult to achieve large group instruction; individual instruction; teacher teaming for efficient use of staff talents; multi-aged grouping; and pupil learning teams. Moreover, the idea of the school as a small replica of society itself is difficult to fulfill. The "eggcrate," while it has, assuredly, served a useful purpose in its time, must be renovated, revitalized and, where possible, replaced. And certainly, when building a new plant, that type of structure should be avoided.

While many forward-thinking educators agree that many or all innovative concepts should be implemented, there is no unanimity as to the exact formula for implementation and there are no set solutions to these problems, hence there is a specific need for educators and boards of education to clearly describe in educational specifications their program requirements, and for building committees and architects to seek new solutions to meeting those requirements in other than the typical, unimaginative schoolhouse.

The educational philosophy. The interdisciplinary middle school must be designed around appropriate educational objectives. In this regard, then, the physical environment will be a vehicle for the program conceived for the children. The educational philosophy hopefully will reflect concern for students' physical and emotional well-being as well as their academic achievement. Yet a most important element in planning the middle school is that educational specifications be developed from a grass roots approach. Too often specifications are developed in isolation by central office administrators, boards of education, and building committees and imposed upon the professional staff who must live with the result of those specifications. A broad statement of educational philosophy needs to be developed which reflects the goals of the school system. The educational philosophy given here is a good illustration of a program with strong concern expressed for the individual student

The program of a middle or intermediate grade school differs markedly from the self-contained classroom of the elementary school with its emphasis on early skill development, and the in-depth experiences of the senior high school. The middle school pre-adolescent, emerging from his childhood years, should have an opportunity to extend his learning horizons through a multitude of wide and varied exploratory experiences. Through these experiences, he can develop further and apply the learning skills, concepts, and early personal values obtained in the elementary school and obtain greater knowledge of those factors and skills which may influence his later life.

To become an effective and contributing member of our social order, it is essential that each student recognize not only his self-worth and potential, but gain an understanding of desirable human relationships through a respect for the abilities, values, and attitudes of others.

The educational program must be designed to recognize and provide for the uniqueness of the individual. His physical, social, emotional, and intellectual differences must be considered. The program must encourage creativity and respect the aspirations, the achievements, the interests, and the rates of learning and maturation of each individual child. In essence, the focus of the school must be centered completely on the individual student. Learning experiences must be purposeful and organized to enable students to discover for themselves through critical thinking those concepts, meanings, and understandings which will contribute to a satisfying adult life. The learning experiences must also help him gain a personal appreciation of his American heritage, a respect for and loyalty to the principles of a democratic society and responsible citizenship, and an insight into the value of continuing education in the world in which he will live.

The curriculum in the middle school should not be considered an end in itself since it must be flexible and dynamic to enable the pupil to meet expanding and changing social and cultural demands of a complex technological age.

Concomitant with the focus on the learner and his differences, the educational program must be designed to recognize and provide for the interaction of teachers in the various disciplines and for close teacher-student personal involvement.[2]

New architectural arrangements. The educational program of the middle school points the way for the kind of architectural arrangements needed. It would be helpful, for example, to develop a building philosophy which will allow for the implementation of the educational philosophy. The Branford position is a good illustration of this:

The average life of a school building in our country at the present time is approximately seventy-five years. With land availability diminishing and through the employment of better construction techniques and materials, it is not unrealistic to assume that newer school buildings will be in use for longer periods of time.

A school building constructed now in Branford will, in all probability, be in use in the year 2050, approximately seventy-five years from the time of construction. Some students attending that school will be earning their living during the last half of the twenty-first century and will be adult members of our society during the first half of the twenty-second century.

It is impossible to predict the types of educational programs and the influence of yet-to-be-discovered technological advances which will be in our schools in the next ten years. Notwithstanding the present rate of educational change, which must be strongly considered, predicting the unknown challenge of the year 2050 would be much like predicting the program of today's school in 1892.

Therefore, it is imperative that schools constructed during the last third of this century be in keeping with the demands of contemporary society and yet planned, as much as is humanly possible, to provide the flexibility which transcends, or, at best, includes the most imaginative modern day educational programming and school plant thought.

There are three functions which should be incorporated

2"Educational Specifications for an intermediate Grade School" (Branford, onn.: Branford Public Schools, February, 1968), p. 3.

in the building design: provision for a continuous (un-graded or non-graded) program for all children, provision for maximum teacher inter-action and planning, and a library which will serve as the informational source center of the school for students and teachers.

The building should be designed to permit the implementation of these functions. Specifically, class-room areas should be far larger than traditionally planned areas. These large classrooms should provide for groupings of approximately 100 to 300 students with provision made for sub-groupings of students for different types of learning experiences within the basic grouping or cluster. Provision for teacher planning should include the creation of a facility or facilities where all teachers can work plan, meet, and discuss ideas and problems together and in small groups. Emphasis should be placed not only in creating those conditions whereby teachers can work intra-departmentally, but also inter-departmentally. The library should be the focal point of the school and be a center which will be used by all students during structured and unstructured time. It should also be a facility which is expandable and which has the flexibility to incorporate those technological changes which can be reasonably anticipated in the future.[3]

In order to develop educational specifications which truly mirror the intentions of the school system, and ones which stand the best chances of being actualized, it is important to get significant input from the staff. For instance, educational planners might develop a "working paper" which can be completed by appropriate professional personnel either on an academic discipline basis for highly specialized areas or on an appropriate interdisciplinary basis. A suggested model is given in Appendix II.

It would be profitable if planners involved pupils' input as well when developing educational specifications. A simple form might be devised to ask middle school pupils their advice. They could be asked: "If you were planning a school, what types of things would you include (or delete)"? Then, list a number of areas to which they could respond, such as the following: rooms; corridors; site; school design; facilities and accessories.

Space requirements for flexible programs. The kinds of spaces

---

[3] *Ibid.*, p. 4.

designed and constructed should be determined by the program requirements and should reflect the needs of the school.

Let us consider four elements for which learning spaces must provide in order to realize an open environment for learning:

1. *Flexible Grouping Capability*

Student needs and program requirements may dictate wide variances in grouping patterns. Students therefore may be grouped in any pattern for instruction and the physical plant should not limit flexibility. Indeed, space should be easily arranged to care for either one student or a group of 100. Movable dividers, such as cabinetry, chalk- or tackboard, can provide for necessary space division within an open plan area.

In Figure 3-1, one can see the degree of flexibility available for grouping. This area of the building has a number of learning zones to facilitate a variety of teacher-student and student-student contact. Mobile dividers permit small or large groups of students to meet.

2. *Personal Interaction*

Open plan construction better allows for interaction among pupils and teachers in the learning process. This type of construction facilitates group discussion, team planning and team learning within and across discipline lines. All professional personnel and students should be part of this interactive process. Again, one can see in Figure 3-1 the multiple possibilities available for personal interaction.

In order to facilitate healthy interaction and communication among all persons in the middle school, the location of the operational areas must be considered. The administrative offices, guidance offices, special services and health need to have an appropriate center from which to provide services. These areas should be positioned so that pupils can have easy access to them. In addition, they should be designed so their functions can be consistent with the educational philosophy of the school.

3. *Expandability, Adaptability, and Maximum Space Utilization*

To predict the educational program requirements for the future is indeed a difficult task considering the current rate of educational and technological advancement. Flexible construction, such as open spaces, allows for future expansion and adaptation of most any kind and indeed can be accomplished

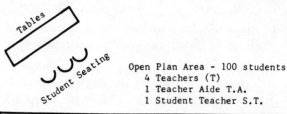

Open Plan Area - 100 students
    4 Teachers (T)
    1 Teacher Aide T.A.
    1 Student Teacher S.T.

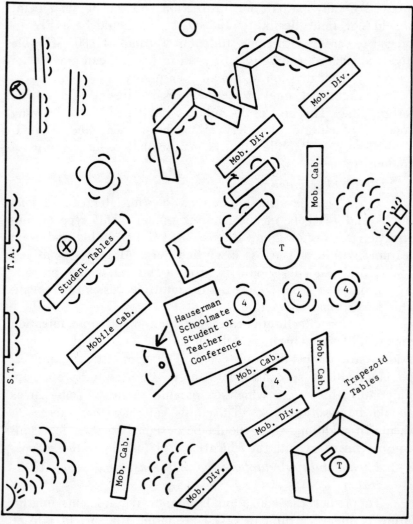

Figure 3-1.

without extensive construction costs. For example, an open environment can be gained by utilizing auditorium space, all purpose rooms, oversized classroom areas, and some corridor space.

Without acoustical treatment, but with removal of fixed seating and provision for movable space dividers, storage and student furniture, a typical school auditorium can be renovated to open spaces for approximately 100 pupils. It is possible to gain over 3,000 square feet of open-plan instructional space in this way.

Similarly, oversized classrooms and all purpose rooms can be converted to open areas where teams of teachers can function with larger clusters of students.

To achieve maximum space utilization is a key responsibility of educational planners.

4. *Easy Access to Instructional Materials Center*

In order not to fragment the learning resources of a school, it is recommended that the instructional materials center be centrally located within the open-plan area so that students and staff have ready access to all materials included therein.

As Figure 3-2 illustrates, the spatial relationship between the instructional materials center and the instructional areas is ideal for facilitating easy flow. Interdisciplinary curriculum building and teaching are easily enhanced by this relationship. Students in a given instructional area, for example, can have immediate access to the instructional materials center to pursue a particular point or interest in his study.

A number of exciting and effective space arrangements are possible in an open-space instructional materials center. In Figure 3-3 it can be seen how equipment and facilities can be arranged in a center which can accommodate about 100 pupils in 4,000 square feet.

Such a center might very well have some of the following facilities and equipment:

A. Seating	B. Shelving
1. "Dry" Carrels	Free standing and Perimeter
2. "Wet" Carrels	shelving for 25,000 volumes
A. C.	
Audio	
Video	

3. Recreational and
    Magazine Reading
4. Group Work Tables

C. Circulation

    Circulation Desk
      2 chairs or stools
      2 book trucks
      1 book deposit truck

D. Reference

    Card Catalog
    Readers Guide Table
    Atlas Stand

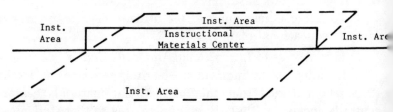

INSTRUCTIONAL MATERIALS CENTER -
CAPABILITIES AND RELATIONSHIPS

Figure 3-2. Instructional materials center — capabilities and relationships.

To facilitate programming and access to materials, an information retrieval system should be included in the instructional center to handle both audio and video program sources, with student respond-record capability where applicable.

The prime function of the list given below is for the preparation and processing of programs for the information retrieval system:

Function	Equipment
Typing	10 Typewriters
Materials Preparation	Counter space
Transparencies	Copier
Posters	Spirit Duplicator
Maps	Reader/Printer
Cut and paste work, etc.	Chalkboard
Small Group Work	
Selection of plays	
Organizing debates, etc.	
Closed Circuit T.V. and Information Retrieval Facility	

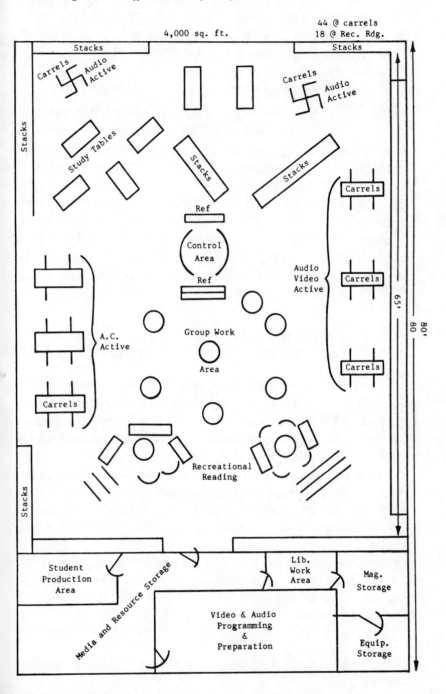

Figure 3-3. Instructional materials center accommodating approximately 100 students.

Control Room
Audio Studio
Television Studio
Retrieval System Storage
Index of Program Sources

Ultimately, the fruits of planning may result in the construction of a middle school facility with infinite possibilities for teaching and learning experiences. The potential for responding to middle school youngsters in more creative ways is enhanced dramatically by an open learning environment. Such a setting has implications for teaching, learning, curriculum, and management.

In the next section of this chapter consideration will be given to the various educational-architectural possibilities suggested by the open-spaces environment which are available for existing plants and facilities.

DEVELOPING INDIVIDUALIZED LEARNING
ENVIRONMENTS IN EXISTING SCHOOLS

Existing conditions. Perhaps the single greatest barrier inherent in using existing educational facilities for individualized learning programs is the lack of variety of spaces and spatial sequence. This limits the opportunities to engage or stimulate individuals or groups in a broad spectrum of activities or experiences.

Most existing facilities have evolved as a response to self-contained, heterogeneously grouped, cellular instruction. As a result, the format usually consists of independent classroom cells joined by a circulation system — traditionally a linear corridor.

Structural systems were used to define these areas through the location of structural walls and columns at the exterior and corridor walls. These blocks of cells were generally further defined by stairs and toilets resulting in predictable zoning patterns. It these blocks of space which are the resources to be reclaimed for new activities.

The major physical implications of individualized learning programs appear to be:

a. Greater variety of group sizes

b. More and smaller group combinations with individual or personal emphasis
c. Greater variety of types of activities
d. Varied degrees of formality in structure of groups
e. Variety and flow of activities (sequence) with an emphasis on the transition or interface of groups or systems
f. Emphasis on the utilization of all experience as education, thus the utilization of all physical environment as learning environment.

It is helpful to consider all the spaces for these activities as being stage sets or theaters which provide the proper mood/setting/environment. Then perhaps one could visualize the interaction of the physical environment with the educational program.

Reorganizing existing facilities (or subdivisions). In order to reorganize existing facilities, it is essential to adopt techniques of subdivision which will yield new patterns and relationships.

Rooms with the long axis perpendicular to the corridor provide the potential for combining two classrooms to permit a group of up to 75 students to gather for lectures, audio-visual or multiple group activities. However, if the long axis of the room is parallel to the corridor, the resultant combined space is too long and narrow for effective single focus activity grouping. (See Figure 3-4.)

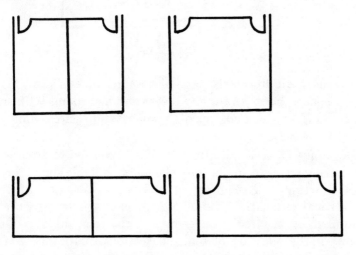

Figure 3-4.

Within a long axis perpendicular to corridor classroom, it is possible to develop two zones within the classroom, thus providing small group study, work, prep, or office space accessible from class or corridor in addition to the medium or standard class. (See Figure 3-5.) These spaces can be particularly effective when glazed all around thus providing maximum inter-group awareness with minimum acoustic distraction.

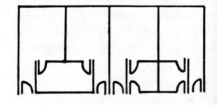

Figure 3-5.

Often group awareness can be encouraged by inserting glazing into existing corridor walls, permitting passing groups or classes opposite to achieve visual contact. It is desirable to omit a corridor partition in order to provide an alcove for study, lounge or display adjacent class and corridor. (See Figure 3-6.)

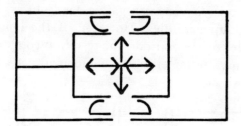

Figure 3-6.

Rooms with long axis parallel to corridor can provide small group spaces by separating two conventional rooms with smaller spaces and, if desired, opening spaces into circulation areas. (See Figure 3-7.)

At times external additions may be required to provide room for greenhouses, circulation elements, outside play, or other class functions. (See Figure 3-8.)

Vertical circulation and awareness can be gained by the addition of internal circulation elements, the removal of sections of floor, or the addition of built-up sections, platforms, frames or stages. The development of multi-level rooms with platforms is an inexpensive device for improving the scale of rooms with

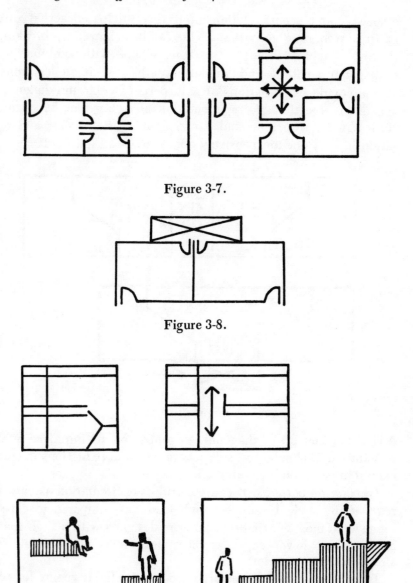

Figure 3-7.

Figure 3-8.

Figure 3-9.

high ceilings or basement rooms with high windows. (See Figure 3-9.)

Often it becomes desirable or necessary to direct or "shape" a space to enhance its relationship to the anticipated activity-use or its surrounding activities. This can be achieved by breaking down the right-angle grid of existing schools with combinations of diagonal partitions and circulation paths at strategic locations. By employing combinations of axis, perpendicular and diagonal, the often objectionable regimentation of rectangular bay structures can be overcome and a variety of spatial effects and relationships can be inexpensively obtained. (See Figure 3-10.)

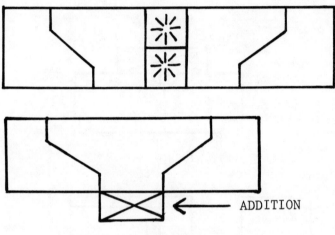

Figure 3-10.

Additional benefits of diagonal reorganization are improved light penetration enhancing outside awareness, and reductions in concentrated partition loads through better load distribution.

Circulation patterns. Because corridors or circulation spaces are required by code to support high loads (as compared to classrooms) and most existing schools were designed with a high load corridor and lower capacity classrooms, it is not possible to simply relocate corridors.

In order to break down large blocks of cellular rooms for replanning, the area to be developed must be rezoned. An example of this would be to consider the row of rooms on each side of a corridor between stairs, toilets or exits — and the corridor to be a zone or suite which has no through traffic. These zones occur in virtually all schools and are predictable in dimension, organization, disposition and frequency. With slab on grade construction the floor structure is not a limitation and it is possible to reroute internal corridors or circulation patterns to provide larger blocks of space uninterrupted by through traffic.

Often the introduction of a new connector or external corridor will permit traffic to be rerouted, reducing congestion and liberating strategic areas for replanning.

By zoning and absorbing the corridor as educational space, new relationships between spaces and activities can be developed which can alter flow and spatial sequence, thus introducing new meaning and experience

If the corridor walls cannot be removed, a core of small activity spaces can be developed from the old corridor providing access to all surrounding areas. If the corridor walls can be removed, a continuous through-building space then becomes available for replanning.

The individual subdivisions—although providing more options than the self-contained cells—are not a complete solution. By grouping subdivisions into suites, the various combinations of spaces, sequences, program groups gain clarification in their relationships within themselves, and to each other, but these suites require clarification to the whole environment that is the school.

Large group spaces. Often existing facilities contain central large group spaces — auditoriums and gymnasia or courtyards. These spaces can often provide the key to reorganization. Generally they are two, and in the case of courtyards three or more stories in height, thus providing access not only to the very heart of the school but at all levels.

If the space was serving as an auditorium, it typically has its main access toward the public entry of the school and seldom provided any classroom or internal relationships. In short, the area was designed for the public and not the student. The standard layout for this space was a formal proscenium auditorium often with fixed seats and a sloped floor. This type of theater space and theater activity is rapidly being abandoned in all levels of dramatic presentation in favor of less rigid organizations providing greater levels of participation and intimacy. The self-contained auditorium is an outgrowth of the self-contained class.

Some auditoriums were constructed as multi-purpose rooms with flat floors and movable furniture but generally had a proscenium stage and, therefore, were limited by this formal format.

In either situation the spaces provide virtually no awareness to the activities in the rest of the building and do little to enhance communication or interaction either through the player-audience relationship or through the activity-school interaction.

Courtyards in general exist to meet natural light requirements and contribute little to the educational program. These spaces vary from multi-story light wells to leftover spaces between long banks of double loaded corridor blocks. Seldom does the court space respond or relate to any class or student activity.

Both types of spaces — courts and auditoriums — can be redeveloped and reshaped to provide new relationships between spaces, areas, and zones within a school which could enhance an educational program. Here awareness and interaction are two key elements in providing a stimulating and responsive environment for the educational activity.

Better relationships between various educational areas in a building can be achieved by redeveloping the auditorium or courtyard as a center of informational exchange and student-faculty interaction. (See Figure 3-11.) This central area can become the place through which the entire school revolves and is resolved.   The community may also become involved within this area.

By opening into the central space at all levels, intergroup awareness can be aided. This can be accomplished in varied degrees according to the educational objectives.

In the case of a courtyard it is possible, through aircondi-

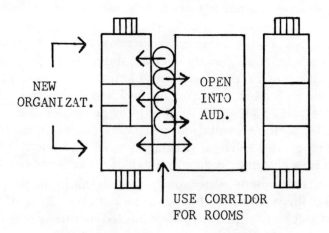

Figure 3-11.

tioning and ventilation, to enclose part of or the entire space to provide a new focus for educational activity.

Outside awareness from within internal or central spaces can be provided through the use of skylights and multilevel penetrations of wells and/or balconies. These devices also permit excellent opportunities for multilevel exhibition, display, and demonstration.

By redeveloping the auditorium space along the lines of an arena theater, the flow from upper levels can be improved as well as the capacity and intimacy of the groupings. Small spaces can be developed under seating areas for storage and study cubicles. (See Figure 3-12.)

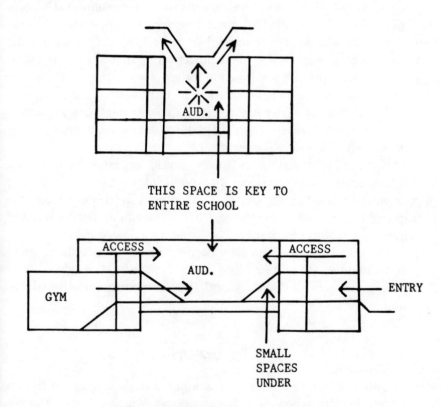

Figure 3-12.

Often it is desirable to provide a multilevel "media" center within a school, and this activity can often be housed within one of these central spaces providing direct access at all levels. "Play spaces" do not necessarily imply large flat floor gymnasium areas, but could easily be organized on multiple level plateaus within a large space. In general terms, any school facility possessing a central or internal court, gym, or auditorium has the potential for being developed into a "loft" type facility.

Relationship of the parts. By subdividing classrooms, rezoning blocks of space, or creating new and redirected foci, an existing facility can gain new meaning and relevance. It is important to remember that the success of any physical environment is a function of all of its parts, which must inevitably include the full sensory spectrum.

A corridor is a communication link. A corridor is a circulation element utilized to connect, separate, and organize similar and dissimilar elements. An an organization-communication element, the corridor provides great educational potential.

A door should be conceived as a link between spaces with the potential for severing the connection; it should be a point of communication—a good location for graphics.

A stair should not be considered only vertical circulation—within a stair the user is directed—aimed toward specific areas. This is conducive to good display-communication for the purpose of stimulation and education.

Entry points and entry areas should be considered as the school-community interface; the point of contact; the meeting or introduction point. These areas should be designed and organized to permit a bridge of academic-social activities and not become a moat, a barrier.

Courts and plazas can provide good places for people to meet and interact, thus providing links extending the educational process into the community and the community into the education process.

SUMMARY

This chapter has suggested a number of procedures to design a new middle school which can accommodate interdisciplinary programs. New architectural arrangements evolve out of educational objectives which in turn reflect the philosophic position of school planners about the educational process. The open concept of space developed in this chapter is intimately connected with the concept of a flexible and open learning environment.

The second part of the chapter centered on the options and alternatives available for redesigning existing plants and facilities to accommodate innovative programs

four

How to interest and
involve the staff

The development of interdisciplinary programs offers unique professional opportunities to organize instructional, curricular and organizational arrangements to fulfill the philosophy of individual self-fulfillment. This means the planning and development of an educational responsibility which will marshal and actualize all the forces needed to execute this philosophy. Moreover, this requires a conscious and purposeful approach which can insure the success of the interdisciplinary program for children.

Therefore, the crucial area of preservice and inservice training must come into focus. To translate the middle school concept into reality is a first order of priority for decision makers. Once teachers and other staff are on the job, there are several questions which must be considered:

1. How can the philosophic commitment, which is the basis of the educational blueprint of the interdisciplinary middle school program, be realized?

2. How can the contribution of new and veteran staff members in the program be maximized?
3. How can teachers, administrators and other personnel be helped to prepare to move to an interdisciplinary middle school from traditional milieus?

INSERVICE EDUCATION: THE PROFESSIONAL DEVELOPMENT RESPONSIBILITY

The nature of inservice training. To many the idea of inservice training is an unexciting event which is probably more ritualistic than beneficial. It is not uncommon for teachers to look upon inservice programs as a series of workshops and seminars which they must attend for the purposes of satisfying school system credit requirements. In many cases this also means attending meetings of professional associations in the hopes of keeping up in the field— Yet this myopic view of inservice training is not what the authors tend to promote nor what they have in mind as an essential component in the success of the interdisciplinary program. What, then, does inservice training mean? As it is developed in this chapter, inservice training applies to the professional development of personnel responsible for carrying out the educational mission of the school. The definition is more than just rhetoric but is conceived as a comprehensive ongoing blueprint which will bring about the achievement of the goals held for children in the middle school. "Ongoing inservice training programs can be a viable way to translate ideas from the talking stage to the operational stage."[1]

The inservice program holds the promise for facilitating changes at all levels of middle school development. In this regard the following guidelines for inservice training are suggested:

1. Inservice training programs need to be continuous if they are to be effective.
2. The programs themselves must be models of enlightened instructional and administrative practices.

---

[1] Philip Pumerantz, "From Idea Stage to Operational Stage: The Inservice Program," *The Middle Grades, Dissemination Services,* Vol. 2, No. 3 (Educational Leadership Institute, Inc.), October, 1970.

3. They must not be haphazard approaches but meaningful, well-planned programs with clearly defined ends put in task oriented terms.
4. They must allow the staff, who will be involved in change, to see the purpose of the idea being promoted. The staff must have the view of the overall operation in which they will be a part
5. The personnel involved must be able to discover for themselves the advantages of the new idea rather than have it handed to them.
6. The inservice program must be learning oriented rather than listening oriented.

It would be instructive to list some types of inservice practices which educators might very well decide to adopt as they get involved in building an innovative school program:

1. Leave policies to encourage and enable teachers to reeducate themselves
2. Visiting professorships to colleges
3. Teacher participation in decision making
4. Teachers' resident study in some facets of life, e.g., industry, art, etc.
5. Residencies following preservice
6. Teacher exchanges within districts, school to school, elementary school to high school, high school to sixth grade, to other schools outside the district.

The purpose of inservice training. Inservice capabilities now offer the possibilities to lift education out of a system of schooling which has not changed fundamentally for decades. The time is appropriate for the evolution of new roles for schools, for teachers and for students. Many have urged that those responsible for the education of children cannot afford to react to change any longer but rather they need to be in the forefront of change.

The interdisciplinary program opens new avenues for reaching and "turning on" all students, and it extends a true new curriculum to respond to the needs of those who are now perhaps neglected. Yet the promise of an interdisciplinary approach will not be realized unless the staff can be prepared to accept this approach.

The change to the interdisciplinary program in the middle school needs to reflect a change in substance and not just a change in form. Educators need to be honest about change and thus it is important that the alternatives which evolve become better than the arrangements which are up for change.

Some of the problems associated with the emergence of the interdisciplinary program in the middle school suggest the basis for the type of inservice training program that should be designed. As is true with a number of new procedures and practices in any field, it is not uncommon to hear teachers and administrators claim that they have no precedent to guide them. Consequently, many tend to blaze trails as they go along. While trail blazing has merit, a helter-skelter, haphazard approach has a number of obvious disadvantages. The purpose of the inservice training program would be to focus on specific training needs in order to fulfill the educational mission of the program.

In addition, inservice training needs to bring teachers and other personnel responsible for the education of children in the interdisciplinary program into focus with contemporary social and educational demands. This means designing training programs which help professionals come to grips with the strengths and weaknesses of current practices in education so that they can make these respond more accurately and meaningfully to children.

DeVita, Pumerantz, and Wilklow suggest two purposes for inservice programs:

1. The how-to-do-it capability, with emphasis on new content and methodology, and
2. Development of positive professional attitudes towards innovation and change.

Here training can focus on getting teachers ready for change and providing opportunities for them to make a change. The real thrust of an inservice program would be to develop within the staff the capability for self-renewal. It is essential in this respect that inservice programs have the continuing machinery to insure that the staff is able to renew and perfect the skills and understandings which would develop over many years.[2]

Planning the inservice program. The training program ultimately is the vehicle to fulfill the promise of the interdisciplinary program. Therefore the components that go into the make-up of inservice training must be themselves models of sound educational practice.

Since the professional development of personnel on the job needs to focus on ways of achieving the ends of the organization, it is important to identify these goals. In order to develop an interdisciplinary program in the middle school, the planners need to take the following steps: assess the need for change based on input from the community, the staff, and the students; identify roadblocks to change; and choose strategies for change which center on ways to overcome the barriers. Once these steps are taken, the inservice training program must be designed to be consistent with the guidelines given above.

Planning the inservice program must be cast, therefore, within the foregoing framework. What questions must be raised in planning a program? Consider the following: Has the need for such training been clearly established? Are the expected outcomes of the program clearly defined? Can these outcomes be met with the present resources? What barriers exist in terms of tradition and policy, etc.? What types of evaluative and monitoring devices should be employed? Finally, what types of follow-through activities will be developed?

One of the most important considerations in a successful professional development program is the establishment of *training purposes.* Once the needs of the educational program have been determined, the process of setting down training objectives emerges.

A. Who will do the training?
B. Are the objectives specific?
C. Are the objectives realistic and attainable?
D. Will the objectives present a challenge?
E. Should a definite time limit be set upon the attainment of the training objectives?

---

[2]Joseph DeVita, Philip Pumerantz, and Leighton Wilklow, *The Effective Middle School* (West Nyack, N.Y.: Parker Publishing Company, 1970), p. 152.

F. Can the training objectives be accomplished without special training of the trainers?

G. Do the training objectives answer "What's in it for me?"

H. Have both long-term, intermediate, and short-term objectives been set?

I. Are there any existing policies or practices that would tend to work against accomplishments of the training objective?"

J. Will the training objectives be reviewed periodically, as progress of the program is measured?

K. Are all members of management who might be affected, informed and in agreement with the objectives of new training program? [3]

A successful initial step in bringing about a change to an innovative program would be to set up a planning workshop involving staff from various schools within the system. Such a workshop could set up a master plan which would establish a chronology. The chronology might cover one to two years' planning and development and would provide for the organization and operation of an interdisciplinary program. It has the advantages of providing the path and direction along which the training can proceed. Out of an initial workshop could come a steering committee or committees with the responsibility for leadership in the evolution of the plan. See Appendix III for a planning model chronology showing a long-range plan developed by Mifflin County School District in Pennsylvania.

Resource consultants could be used at such a workshop to make a presentation on the philosophy and rationale for the middle school and the interdisciplinary program; the nature of the emerging adolescent; descriptions of new practices in teaching, scheduling, organization, and curriculum.

Along with the development of a master plan which covers a long period of time, a rather comprehensive training program which allows for uninterrupted instruction needs to be planned. A summer program in the form of a workshop is one of the most successful.

Ideally, participants should include all personnel who will be involved in the new program, but space and cost restrictions

---

[3]*Dynamic Management* (Addison-Wesley Publishing Co.). Original author unknown.

may prohibit the convening of a large group to be training at one time. To overcome these constraints, and at the same time to facilitate change, a representative group of professional personnel could be brought together for inservice instruction. Out of this endeavor could come several pilot projects which could serve as the "lighthouse" programs to launch the interdisciplinary program. For an example of a proposal for a training program as the one described here, see Appendix IV.

Some expected outcomes. The results of successfully planned inservice training programs can be a source of satisfaction to those who planned and conducted them and to those who participated in them as well. The following proposal was made by a team from a junior high school who had attended an inservice training program which had focused on the development of an interdisciplinary program. This proposal was a rewarding outcome of the training program since its intent was to design, develop and launch a pilot interdisciplinary program in a traditional junior high school and set the stage for a conversion to a middle school.

A Plan to Organize a Pilot Interdisciplinary Program in a Junior High School

To increase the effectiveness of learning program and work out Basic Plan for middle school organization:

1. Organize one multi-disciplinary team for 1970-71 (120 students Grade 7)
2. Utilize maximum flexibility scheduling
3. Develop "Theme" based program, applying stimulating opportunities for learning by utilizing strengths of team members and all available flexible facilities and resource materials

Hale House (An Interdisciplinary Team)
    120 7th Grade Students
        Random Selection
        Fully Heterogeneous
4 Home Rooms
        Staff
        Language Arts ⎫
        Science   ⎬ Theme Development
        Math   ⎭
        Social Studies

Aide	– Clerical and Resource
	– Assistant
Head Teacher	– 1/2 Teacher, 1/2 Administrator
Counselor	– Shared with S.D.P.
Resource Aides	– Community, Department Heads, University Student Teachers

Summer Plans

Conduct 1 week full time workshop for staff in August.
a. Review Concepts
b. Establish Roles
c. Begin Creating List of Themes
d. Write "mini-units" to Explore Themes
e. Assign Facilities and Create Schedule[4]

Another example of the type of interest which can be generated on the part of participants is shown by the plans one group developed at the workshop discussed above. This group recommended that the staff in their school participate in the following activities in the coming year·

1. Visit existing middle schools which have sucessfully demonstrated individualized programs.
2. Have the staff meet with consultants and others who are conversant with cooperative teaching and individualized instruction.
3. Determine whether the present plant can house inter-disciplinary-type programs.
4. Make some meaningful decisions about the goals of the instructional program at the end of grade 8 in the light of considering a theme-based interdisciplinary program.
5. One afternoon a week should be used by teachers who have mutual concerns about students so they can discuss and plan ways to resolve such problems.

Frequently participants of successful workshops feel that heir experiences have been important as an exercise in ini-

---

[4]A Plan to Organize a Pilot Interdisciplinary Program in Nathan Hale Junior 1igh School, Norwalk, Connecticut, Summer, 1970. (Mimeographed.)

tiating thinking about ways to plan valid programs for students. Some of the following comments capture the type of impact the one-week experience in Norwalk had on teachers, guidance counselors, and administrators who participated:

> The idea of teachers working together whether in strict subject disciplines or in interdisciplinary structure is important.
>
> I felt the excitement of something new coming into existence and I'm glad I was and will be a part of it.
>
> A desire to meet again for a progress report of things discussed in the workshop.
>
> A desire for more faculty discussions, field trips, and consultants.
>
> Implementation of the interdisciplinary approach with the support of all available resources.
>
> A desire for more discussion with children.
>
> A desire to have mini workshops.
>
> A desire to have meetings to share information, particularly where teams have been organized and are functioning.
>
> The most significant and important look at a better way to reach children.
>
> It was good to be recharged again.

Sustaining the momentum. Once an inservice program has been launched and momentum has been generated, people can start to discover some of the exciting new approaches dealing with teaching and learning. When this point is reached, a number of activities should be undertaken and supported by the educational leaders. Some of these activities might be as follows:

1. Give maximum support to the pilot program being developed in the school.

2. Encourage and support the use of university-based student teachers in the innovative programs. This may include providing for a number of interns in a building during a semester. It would be helpful in terms of organizing research studies where experimental and control groups would be necessary.

3. Encourage and support the conduct of research studies in

the innovative schools along lines that will yield data for nationwide as well as local replication. For example, the following hypotheses might very well be advanced and tested:

a. In the interdisciplinary program, pupils will show greater gains on standardized achievement tests than pupils of the same grades in non-interdisciplinary programs.

b. In the interdisciplinary program, significant changes in teacher roles and attitudes can be observed and documented.

c. In the interdisciplinary program, pupils will show greater gains on self-concept inventories than pupils of the same grades in non-middle schools.

d. Student teachers training in an interdisciplinary team will show significant changes in attitudes than student teachers in a more conventional arrangement.

4. Explore and encourage the arrangement of exchange teaching possibilities between teachers in successful middle schools in other locations.

5. Make use of teacher planning days which may be available in a system. Plan a variety of inservice programs to promote innovations already generated.

INSERVICE STRATEGIES AND VEHICLES

To convert the intentions of educational planners into viable workable arrangements means using techniques in training which will actualize these intentions. It must be kept in mind that inservice training is a vehicle to fulfill educational goals. In this regard, then, let us turn to a consideration of several successful strategies for inservice training.

Simulation. One of the most effective training approaches which combines the advantages of an interesting setting and the possibilities of skill development is simulation. When it is important to put people into the roles of other groups whose life style and experiences they have never had, simulations come in handy. For example, to have teenagers try to discover the intricacies and variables of parenthood or to have teachers develop insights into the roles of students, one might very well use simulation games. Let us consider now some of the features of simulation games as a basis for their use in training.

First, simulation requires a great deal of involvement on the part of the participants. In this regard, whatever one does, whatever decision one makes, it becomes immediately apparent. These moves then have a good chance of making an impact on the person involved; that is, each participant tends to be his own evaluator and judge since his actions are quite personalized Each is in the position of actualizing a behavior rather than simply talking about it, and in this sense can make a meaningful move. As one is forced to act, one has the opportunity to observe the nature and hopefully the quality of his behavior.

In inservice training, simulation can revolve around a number of problem inputs. These problems can be taken from information derived from the staff and then a program using simulation can be built around such inputs.

A number of commercially developed simulation games are available for use in inservice training programs.

Case studies. How does one interest and involve the staff in the development of an interdisciplinary program? Typically this question arises when the implementation of an innovation is considered. How does one transmit the excitement he possesses about the operation to staff members and other colleagues? How does one promote the interdisciplinary idea? How does one get teachers to agree to alter and improve their teaching styles and methodology? A very effective device to use in bringing about change is the case study. Such an approach is relatively simple to devise for use in a faculty meeting or a series of inservice meetings or as part of a more complete and comprehensive professional development program. Basically a case study involves background information relative to a particular setting. It includes a description of roles involved, the setting, etc. The case study approach is more structured than simulation since most of the dialogue has been given and the participant does not have the freedom in choosing a course of action as he might have with simulations. Notwithstanding, case studies can be very effective in placing people in situations which can help develop insights and other decision-making skills.

To meet some of the questions raised above, one might develop homemade case studies to deal with a particular problem. For example, while trying to help teachers alter teacher attitudes relative to new ideas, a case study might very well involve the dimensions of the problem case in a familiar situation. In this case, teachers could be asked to play the role of the principal trying to bring about change, and the role of other teachers resisting change. Following the act, the participants could be asked to identify the nature of the problem and its underlying causes and to compare their thinking with that of their colleagues. Through a question-and-discussion session the problem can be analyzed and then hopefully insights developed which might be a significant step forward in dealing with the problem.

Sensitivity training. Of late the idea of sensitivity training has come under a great deal of fire from many quarters of the lay and professional community. Misunderstanding and difficult-to-measure outcomes have raised these doubts. Yet sensitivity training is a vehicle which can promote skill development in human interaction. Sensitivity training provides for and indeed requires a very high degree of involvement and participation by those in the sessions.

Competent and well trained group leaders are essential, though, to carry out a sensitivity training program. People who possess such skills are not difficult to locate. Such training is designed to help participants discover a number of things about themselves through open and frank encounters with other participants, and hopefully as a result, to be able to understand others and thus communicate more effectively with them. Through the development of healthy interfaces there may come cooperation and understanding and the accomplishment of educational goals.

Clearly, faulty interpersonal relationships can cause frustration and dissatisfaction within a school, and this can become a serious barrier to the successful implementation of an interdisciplinary program. Therefore, the improvement of human relations skills should receive a high priority in planning for professional improvement. Often the pressures of teaching and administration tend to hold people captives in their roles, with little chance to step outside and view their relationships with others, and hence little opportunity to alter their attitudes. Therefore, the inclusion of sensitivity training in inservice programs can provide teachers, guidance counselors, administrators and others with important human relations skills.

Communication. The development of new learning models and teaching models which are consistent with the prescriptive type of teaching required in an interdisciplinary program can cause a number of difficulties for teachers. Learning is a process of behavioral change and it takes place in a number of ways. For the most part, learning in school results from interpersonal relationships between the student and the teacher in the environment in which the teacher has provided for the student. In this setting exist the conditions in which the learner will order and reorder data and ideas into meaningful patterns. This, then, requires open avenues of communication. Teachers and students, teachers and administrators, and teachers and teachers need to talk to each other. Frequently, however, each is anxious to offer his own message while unaware of the effect his delivery is having upon the recipient. Inservice training programs can focus on this need to improve communication. In this regard such programs must be concerned with three components which constitute the intercommunication network: (1) the milieu in which communication takes place, (2) the attitudes of the parties involved, and (3) the resultant behaviors.

An inservice program could profitably offer role-playing situations where participants can begin to examine the reasons for faculty communication and the reasons which may impede learning. What may become apparent from such activity is the awareness of the effect people have on each other. Such experience should suggest a number of ways to develop awareness of others in the hopes of facilitating communication.

An excellent device in training would be to video-tape a role-playing act and replay it for the participants. Such a play could represent one of a number of options available in opening channels of communication. After the participants have had a chance to watch the video-tape and listen to the reactions of their colleagues to the play, discussion of the different ways in which the matter could have been handled might very well be carried out. Perhaps, following this discussion, one member of the group might present another situation for discussion which was a source of difficulty to him and to others.

Seminar-workshops. The seminar workshop can be the vehicle which can assist teachers and other staff in developing the skills necessary to carry out the interdisciplinary program. Here the various training strategies may be employed. Some workshop topics which teachers need to consider are the following: working with the slow learner and low achiever; teaching discovery lessons; enrichment instruction; working with small groups; individualizing and personalizing instruction; and using instructional media.

This is conceived as an on-site working program which could last from one day to several months. In a workshop, for example, teachers may be involved in concurrent demonstration teaching sessions. In this case teachers could spend one afternoon a week[5] observing a demonstration by one or more master teachers in some particular methodology or curriculum theme area. As Figure 4-1 illustrates, each demonstration can last about twenty minutes (more or less, depending on the time available) so that the participants can move to another demonstration center for another twenty-minute session. This scheme can be continued about three times in an afternoon, thus giving each person the opportunity to observe three different approaches. Hopefully this type of activity will provide teachers with a number of excellent teaching styles and different ways to utilize materials.

Another approach is a program developed with the cooperation of a college or university which responds to the specific training needs of the middle school. Such an arrangement could be of one or more days' duration and scheduled at the convenience of the participants. One might consider it a workshop or a course, but whatever one decides to label it, it can do some of the following: (a) provide the broad background for the philosophy of the middle school and the interdisciplinary approach, (b) give attention to the operational needs in implementing the middle school, and (c) bring a prescriptive experience to the participants based on a diagnostic experience. That is, the program could be centered around specific operational problems such as the development of teams in the interdisciplinary program, which the participants can study through a simulation process (Figure 4-1).

Instructors or consultants can work closely with school system personnel in helping to develop the skills necessary to carry out the educational program.

Inservice evaluation. It is important that attention be focused on the area of evaluation. A very successful program requires that all aspects of training be scrutinized to see the areas of

---

[5]A variety of time arrangements could be developed for the convenience of the staff and obviously should not be rigid.

Concurrent Demonstration Teaching Sessions

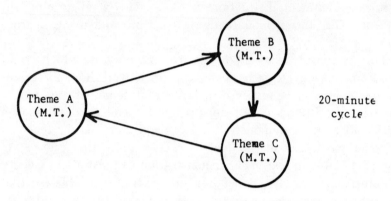

One or more master teachers (M.T.) will be in each
center demonstrating how to teach in a particular curriculum area.

Figure 4-1.

strength and the areas of weakness. Efforts should be made to
involve the staff in the evaluation while it is in progress and
also at its conclusion. A participant evaluation committee, working with the inservice program directors, should be encouraged
to help to devise instruments for measuring the effectiveness of
the program in process and its outcomes. Such instruments
could indicate the possible changes to be made in the instruction. In addition to an on-going monitoring evaluation, a final
evaluation should also be undertaken.

A necessary technique should be the follow-up survey to determine the effectiveness of the training program in terms of
meeting the stated objectives. The feedback from such follow-up
evaluation could be used to develop objectives for the on-going
self-renewal in which the participants should be involved.

These evaluations should apply to every type of inservice program whether it be a one-day session or a session of several
months' duration.

SOME PROFESSIONAL DEVELOPMENT MODELS

It would be helpful at this point to suggest some models
which could be used as part of the professional development

program of a middle school. The models offered here could be replicated in whole or various components of it can be adapted to fit the unique situation of various schools and school systems. But before turning to successful inservice plans, we will outline the important dimensions of such plans. Guidelines which serve to provide the proper directions for the training program need to be established. This direction includes general objectives and the specific outcomes desired, as well as a determination of the areas of study.

Guidelines for converting to an interdisciplinary program. A professional development program might very well have as its theme the self-fulfillment of the individual. As such, a number of general objectives might be appropriate, such as the following:

1. The achievement of a quality of instruction in which the idea of individualized instruction becomes more than just rhetoric but reality in terms of the interests, needs and lives of pre- and early adolescents.
2. The identification of the constantly changing needs in the operation of a middle school.
3. The expansion of the insight and understanding of teaching middle school children, and identification of the gaps of knowledge and the problem areas which need to be dealt with in a self-renewal program.
4. The development of a model educational program which can serve as a vision for the staff.

Upon the completion of a professional development program, one might assume that each participant should be able to perform the following specific tasks:

1. Write a philosophy that shows a commitment to educational innovation and change
2. Identify the characteristics of the pre- and early adolescent in social, physical, and psychological terms
3. Develop a learning program which is based on the principles of child growth and development
4. Construct a curriculum which breaks out of the confines of departments and combines *basic academic skills* and *basic human relations skills* in one learning package or unit

5. Select appropriate prepared learning materials which will facilitate individualized instruction
6. Evaluate learning materials from commercial sources by using guidelines shown to be successful in the field
7. Develop in-class learning materials which will facilitate individualized instruction
8. Evaluate in-class learning materials by using guidelines shown to be successful in the field
9. Identify various ways in which community resources can enhance the curriculum themes
10. Construct instruments and design procedures which will give data about a teacher's ability to teach and a student's ability to learn
11. Construct instruments and design procedures which will give data about the capability of the program as a whole
12. Use prepared instruments to get data about teaching, learning, and program
13. Translate the findings derived from various data-gathering sources about teaching, learning, and programs into procedures aimed at bringing about change in these areas.

A number of areas of study may be used as components of an effective professional development program. The following list provides some excellent guidelines for focusing the training program on professional and institutional self-renewal:

1. The nature of the pre- and early adolescent
2. Teacher awareness and fostering positive self-perception on the part of students
3. Communicating with pre- and early adolescents
4. Uses of community resources in curriculum development
5. Developing and writing interdisciplinary themes
6. Helping teachers develop their own appropriate teaching materials
7. Evaluating teaching, learning, and programs
8. Simulation and role-playing in interdisciplinary teaching
9. Diagnostic and prescriptive teaching to achieve individualization
10. Writing behavioral objectives
11. Verbal and nonverbal interaction
12. Methods of individualizing instruction.

Inservice programs. What should emerge from the establishment of the guidelines is an inservice training program which can focus on the objectives outlined. Appendix IV is an illustration of a one-week program based on the guidelines suggested above. This program would be most effectively handled in a summer and is designed to accommodate approximately thirty participants. The reader will note that the participants are divided into three groups and each group spends a block of time with an instructor(s) on a given topic and then rotates to another instructor and topic. In this way each group spends a relatively long period of time with each instructor (a whole morning or more). The authors' experience with this approach has been quite successful in that participants are involved in more interaction with the instructor and fellow participants; that is, the longer block of time lends itself to less lecturing and more doing.

SUMMARY

This chapter has considered the strategies and techniques educators need to translate middle school concept into reality. Attention here has been focused on the purposes for inservice training and the ways to plan inservice programs. A number of practical ideas have been put forward regarding the development of inservice programs and strategies. Finally several inservice models have been suggested to assist educators in converting to interdisciplinary programs.

five

How to schedule
interdisciplinary programs

There is no simple formula for scheduling interdisciplinary programs. Local school conditions, problems, and the extent of commitment to this type of instruction are all factors to be considered.

Since an interdisciplinary approach essentially involves the manner in which teachers of various disciplines interact, it is important that the schedule provide framework for both flexibility and planning. The basic factors necessary for a sound schedule-structure are:

1. Adequate planning time
2. Flexibility in structure
3. Staff-space utilization.

PLANNING TIME FOR THE STAFF

It may surprise some that planning time is enumerated as the first, and possibly most important, principle. However, the teacher and the teacher-team can function within the interdisciplinary framework only as a result of adequate planning and dialogue. The vitality inherent in an interdisciplinary presentation results only after a significant process of mutual planning, preparation, and sharing of strategies. The traditional "free period" as preparation time cannot meet the demands necessary of this type of team-teaching. The schedule must provide for a block of time in which four of the five team members plan their unit or approach together. This obviously requires that other staff members must have their programs organized accordingly, allowing appropriate coverage for students.

As a consequence, the sample schedules (Tables 1 and 2) generally allow adequate time for joint planning and individual research or preparation. The back-to-back nature of sequential block, versus problems-oriented humanities block, creates possibilities for either group of teachers to spend up to 25 percent of any day in preparation or research. The concept of research and preparation on school time has never been fully dev oped in the public school. This is often the result of teacher assignment for purposes of student accounting and coverage. Yet the demands of our changing academic scene, as well as the team concept, are requiring us to take a second look at this problem. We believe that some of the proposed approaches to scheduling provide definite solutions to these questions.

FLEXIBILITY IN STRUCTURE

Interdisciplinary teaching can evolve as a series of unit-type activities. The schedule should provide the framework for movement into units or "problems," and then back to a more self-contained, traditional program. The breather spaces between units provide for both follow-up and the opportunity for developing additional units. The development of unit themes or problems requires the preparation mentioned previously. Follow-up and unit reviews can proceed here also.

Viable programs cannot function in the atmosphere restricted by schedules whose primary purpose is administrative convenience. The schedule must be thought of as a series of blocks. Within each block, activities occur in a fluid and dynamic way. The nature of each block is determined by the disciplines involved

TABLE 1

PLANNING AND PREPARATION TIME FOR 6TH, 7TH, OR 8TH GRADE *HUMANITIES* TEAMS FUNCTIONING WITHIN AN INTERDISCIPLINARY MASTER SCHEDULE

(ENGLISH, SOCIAL STUDIES, SCIENCE, MATH, OR ARTS)

Time	Module	Period	6	7	8
8:20	1 2	1			
9:00	3 4	2	Teaching	Planning and Research	Teaching
9:40	5 6	3			
10:20	7 8	4		Teaching	
11:00	9 10	5	Planning and Research		Lunch and Supervision
11:40	11 12	6		Lunch and Supervision	Planning and Research
12:20	13 14	7	Lunch and Supervision		
1:00	15 16	8		Teaching	
1:40	17 18	9	Teaching		Teaching
2:20	19 20	10	Teaching (Personal Development)	Teaching	Teaching

within it, and in a practical way, by the facilities and space available at a given time. For example, the humanities block might at one time encompass social studies, English, science, and math. The students' involvement in various levels of instruction can be regulated by flexible regrouping within the block. Heterogeneously grouped students can, at any time, be moved from one discipline into another and then back again. A hypothetical situation is presented as an example.

TABLE 2

PLANNING AND PREPARATION FOR SPECIFIC
DISCIPLINES WITHIN THE *SEQUENTIAL TEAM*

(MATH REPLACES MUSIC OR ART IF PRO-
GRAMMED AS A SEQUENTIAL SUBJECT)

Period	Phys. Ed.	Music or Art	Foreign Language
1	Teaching 7	Planning 7	Teaching 7
2		Teaching 7	Planning 7
3	Planning 7		Teaching 7
4	Teaching 6	Planning 6, 8	Teaching 6
5		Teaching 6	Planning 6, 8
6	Planning 6		Teaching 6
7	Lunch	Lunch	Lunch and Superv.
8	Teaching 8	Teaching 8	Teaching 8
9			Teaching (Personal Development)
10	Teaching (Personal Development)	Ensembles	Teaching 8

Let us assume there are one hundred students who are to be
assigned heterogeneously into four disciplines meeting in a block
divided into four teaching periods. We might proceed as follows:

I. Divide students into groups of five, assigning a number or letter to each group. Each group can be homogeneous, heterogeneous, or combined for some specific reason, such as math ability.

A	B	C	D
Jones			
Smith			
Lee	5 Students	5 Students	5 Students
Williams			
Peters			

E	F	etc.
5 Students	5 Students	

II. Combine groups as follows, dividing the alphabet equally through period 1, and rotate accordingly (Table 3).

TABLE 3

FOUR PERIOD BLOCK

	Period 1	Period 2	Period 3	Period 4
English	ABFGH	CDEIJ	STMNO	KOPQR
Science	CDEIJ	ABFGH	KLPQR	STMNO
Social Studies	KLPQS	MNORT	ABHIJ	FGCDE
Math	MNORT	KLPQS	FGCDE	ABHIJ

If music or art teachers are added to the team for purposes of integrative activities, the total time block might be temporarily altered by combining two disciplines into a larger unit and adding the third teacher (Table 4).

The music teacher can simply move into either class and meet all students over the four periods. This either relieves the regular

TABLE 4

COMBINING ENGLISH AND SOCIAL STUDIES,
AND ADDING A MUSIC OR ART TEACHER

	Period 1	Period 2	Period 3	Period 4
English	ABFGH	CDEIJ	STMNO	KLPQR
Social Studies	KLPQS	MNORT	ABHIJ	FGCDE

teacher or provides for division into subgroups. An alternate possibility is to form a third station, removing some children from both classes, however allowing them to receive instruction in all three areas over the two-day period. This is illustrated over a five-day period (Table 5)

TABLE 5

MONDAY, WEDNESDAY, FRIDAY				
	Period 1	Period 2	Period 3	Period 4
English	ABF	CDE	STMNO	KLPQR
Social Studies	KLP	MNO	ABHIJ	FGCDE
Music	GHQS	IJRT		

TUESDAY, THURSDAY				
	Period 1	Period 2	Period 3	Period 4
English	GH	IJ	STMNO	KLPQR
Social Studies	QS	RT	ABHIJ	FGCDE
Music	ABFKLP	CDEMNO		

Music classes on Monday, Wednesday, and Friday were developed by extrapolating the last two letters of each group; on Tuesday and Thursday, by rotating the first three of each remaining group. During the second week, the same format can be implemented into Periods 3 and 4 instead, to allow the Periods 1 and 2 groups the resumption of regular instruction in social studies and English.

If both art and music were being incorporated into the program, it is possible that art could be introduced into Periods 3 and 4 in a similar manner, while music was being taught during Periods 1 and 2.

Another possibility is offered here. The small class size remaining creates opportunities for combining English and social studies into larger groups, providing further interrelationships. One of the two remaining teachers can then be released to work with small enrichment or remedial groups (Table 6).

TABLE 6

MONDAY, WEDNESDAY, FRIDAY

	Period 1	Period 2
English	Remedial group	Enrichment group
Social Studies	ABFKLP (Interdisciplinary Activity)	CDEMNO
Music	GHQS	IJRT

Thus far we have discussed more formal block structures. Many teams can incorporate programs within an extremely loose-knit time block which provides for no more structure than student accounting. Students are located in a certain place at a specific time, with team activities "following" generated activities and developing units in an informal way. This is usually desirable for a short-term unit which follows a definite theme, i.e., "Environment." It can also involve field work or pragmatic activities. Table 7 is based upon a unit involving three groups of forty 7th graders under the supervision of four teachers.[1]

---

[1] Suggested by a seventh grade Interdisciplinary Unit. Fox Lane Middle School, Bedford, N.Y., 1969.

TABLE 7

	Room 3	Room 4	Room 5
8:00 - 9:00	ABFGHCDE	MNORTKUS	KLPQRIJH
9:00 - 11:00	MNORTKUS	KLPQRIJH	ABFGHCDE

STAFF, SPACE UTILIZATION

The examples presented here are based upon a hypothetical program, but they serve to illustrate possibilities applicable to the typical school. The authors proceed here upon the assumption that the majority of middle schools operate on the "House Plan," and separate the student body into three equal divisions. Each house or division contains an identical 6th, 7th, and 8th grade student body, usually remaining in the same house over the three-year period. This usually results in the opportunity for two grade levels to receive instruction in the house, while the third is involved in central facilities, housing, physical education, shop or music. This arrangement has worked well, but has not been consistent with the interdisciplinary rationale. There results a tendency to further separate and delineate "academic subjects" opposed to the "special subjects," often because of the fact that both are necessarily taught in two distinct environments. Also, there is more here than physical separation of the two staffs. The academic teacher bears a different status and relationship with the student than does the "specialist," often with an unfortunate loss of academic integrity on the part of the musician, craftsman, or artist.

This problem has been discussed sufficiently, but now we must face the realities of physical space utilization and effective assignment of staff members.

Some basic questions evolve at this point. If the intent is to bring additional personnel into the academic situation, the following factors should be considered.

1. Will this involve a switching of teachers to insure that each other's areas are covered?
2. Do we expand the team by temporarily or permanently adding the new teacher? If so, who covers his previous responsibilities?
3. Is the crisscrossing of lines of responsibilities and disciplines a structured and well-organized procedure, or should flexibility be maintained, enabling involvement of personnel at strategic times? How much do we involve administration here?
4. Since it is desirable that we maintain the specific integrity of the special areas, what proportion of the students' time should be spent in specific involvement in the fine, manual, or performing arts?
5. Will our teachers respond negatively to the possibilities of movement into instructional areas foreign to themselves, i.e., presenting an English lesson in the shop area? Can their lessons be more effective? Can we limit the extent to which teachers must change instructional areas?

The authors will attempt to provide answers to these questions through a discussion of various scheduling techniques. Some have been adopted from various interdisciplinary middle school programs. A study will be made of the master schedule either as it would relate to one house of a two- or three-house middle school, or as a total small middle school. The following student body and staff numbers are typical and are used for purposes of example.

    I.   108 Children at each grade level

    II. Personnel   1 Teacher in Charge or Administrative
       (6, 7, 8)   Assistant
                  1 Guidance Counselor
                  3 English Teachers
                  3 Math
                  3 Science

3 Social Studies
1 Music
1 Art
2 Foreign Language

III. Shared Personnel:
Home Economics
Shop
Physical Education
Remedial Reading
Nurse
Paraprofessionals (2)
Librarian

IV. Classroom Areas:
At any given time, space to accommodate two grade levels in the academic disciplines which include
English
Social Studies
Math
Foreign Language
Science
The third grade level is involved in shared facilities or special classroom areas:
Music
Art
Shop, Home Economics
Physical Education
This formula is subject to variation if music were alternated with math, etc.

Table 8 would accommodate these facilities or variations of it.

Since the *Humanities Block* allows for movement without much special facilities use, students can be scheduled without too much difficulty (Table 9).

The music or art teacher can rotate through any portion of this at times that correlated activities are introduced.

The *Sequential Block* presents more specific restrictions. Based upon Table 9, the Sequential Block can be arranged as in Tables 10 to 15 (for purposes of identification, each grade level is divided into four equal alphabetical groups, A, B, C, and D).

TABLE 8

A BASIC MASTER SCHEDULE WHICH ALLOWS FOR
TWO-THIRDS IN-HOUSE SPACE UTILIZATION

Time	Period	6	7	8
8:15	1 / 2 — 1	HUMANITIES	SEQUENTIAL	HUMANITIES
8:55	3 / 4 — 2	English		
9:35	5 / 6 — 3	Social Studies / Math / Science		
10:15	7 / 8 — 4	SEQUENTIAL	HUMANITIES	
10:55	9 / 10 — 5	Physical Education / Arts		LUNCH
11:35	11 / 12 — 6	Foreign Language	LUNCH	HUMANITIES
12:15	13 / 14 — 7	LUNCH		
12:55	15 / 16 — 8	HUMANITIES	HUMANITIES	SEQUENTIAL
1:35	17 / 18 — 9			
		PERSONAL DEVELOPMENT – ELECTIVES		

Shop (Home Economics) can rotate to allow for alternate double periods (Table 13). Art activities can more easily be implemented into the Humanities block, consequently the shorter period here. Another possibility which makes use of extended periods is to schedule Home Economics/Shop for one-half year, art for the other.

Another possibility is to develop a master schedule which allows for movement into areas of non-gradedness. Table 15 combines 7th and 8th grade Humanities Blocks. Additionally, it places math in both the Humanities and Sequential blocks, making provision for a back-to-back schedule. This allows for a non-graded math continuum.

TABLE 9

ROOM UTILIZATION FOR THE *HUMANITIES*
BLOCK ACCORDING TO THE TABLE 8 MASTER
SCHEDULE, USING TWO-THIRDS OF
STUDENT BODY IN HOUSE

Period	Room 1 English	2 English	3 Social Studies	4 Social Studies	5 Math	6 Math	7 Science	8 Science
1	6	8	6	8	6	8	6	8
2	6	8	6	8	6	8	6	8
3	6	8	6	8	6	8	6	8
4	7	8	7	8	7	8	7	8
5	7	X	7	X	7	X	7	X
6	X	8	X	8	X	8	X	8
7	8	7	8	7	8	7	8	7
8	6	7	6	7	6	7	6	7
9	6	7	6	7	6	7	6	7

This arrangement places art or music in the Humanities block and allows for some math students from one level to move into the alternate grade level. The extent to which this could be implemented is restricted by space factors and those specific facilities existing in the local school situation.

INDIVIDUALIZING INSTRUCTION

While our schedule provides the framework for placement of students into workable curricular divisions, there must be an orderly process of designating students into areas of personal need. Some of the methods through which this can be achieved are familiar:

Remedial groups   Contracts
Enrichment groups   Field studies
Independent study

TABLE 10

SEQUENTIAL TEACHING SCHEDULE ACCORDING TO
THE PREVIOUS BASIC MASTER SCHEDULE

Period	6					7					8				
	Ph. Ed.	Art	Mus.	Shop H.Ec.	For. Lang.	Ph. Ed.	Art	Mus.	Shop H.Ec.	For. Lang.	Ph. Ed.	Art	Mus.	Shop H.Ec.	For. Lang.
1						AB	C			CD					
2	AB					AB		C	D						
3	AB	C							D	AB					
4					CD										
5				D	AB										
6			C	D											
7											AB				
8											AB	C		D	CD
9													C	D	CD

TABLE 11

SEQUENTIAL TEACHING SCHEDULE – ALTERNATE DAYS

Period	6					7					8				
	Ph. Ed.	Art	Mus.	Shop H.Ec.	For. Lang.	Ph. Ed.	Art	Mus.	Shop H.Ec.	For. Lang.	Ph. Ed.	Art	Mus.	Shop H.Ec.	For. Lang.
1						CD				AB					
2						CD	A		B						
3								A	B	CD					
4	CD				AB										
5	CD	A		B											
6			A	B	CD										
7											CD				AB
8											CD	A		B	
9													A	B	CD

TABLE 12

SEQUENTIAL ACTIVITIES FOR ANY GRADE
LEVEL ON A DAILY BASIS FOR TWO WEEKS

REPEAT AT THE BEGINNING OF THE THIRD WEEK

Period	M	T	W	Th	F	M	T	W	Th	F
1	PE	Lang.	PE	Lang.	PE	Lang.	PE	Lang.	PE	Lang.
2	PE	Mus.	PE	Art	PE	Mus.	PE	Shop	PE	Mus.
3	Lang.	Shop	Lang.	Art	Lang.	Art	Lang.	Shop	Lang.	Art

Refer to Chapter II for a discussion of the rationale and function of each of these. However, attention here is centered on
methods of scheduling them.

REMEDIAL- ENRICHMENT GROUPS

Excepting remedial reading, which is usually administered by
a specialist, relatively large groups of children are in need of
developmental or supportive help in areas of reading and math.
Many critics of team- and interdisciplinary-teaching hold that
too much emphasis is placed upon conceptualization, and too
little upon basic skills development. On the contrary, the block
period and personal development concept provide many avenues
for emphasis upon basic skills. A review of the previous Humani-
ties-Block schedule examples will indicate the availability of
additional staff at various times, in addition to possibilities of
expansion into and out of larger and smaller groups. Specific
teachers, being scheduled back to back, can depart with smaller
clusters of students into both remedial or enrichment groups.
This is especially possible during the Humanities Block. Non-
foreign language students meeting during the sequential block
are often in need of basic language or math skills. Humanities-
Block teachers available on a rotating basis can be assigned
to assist here. While this affects some of their planning time, it
is possible to make reasonable adjustments on a rotating basis.

TABLE 13

A *SEQUENTIAL BLOCK* WHICH ALLOWS FOR MATH, IN PLACE OF ART OR MUSIC, ASSUMING THAT THE LATTER HAVE BEEN MOVED INTO THE *HUMANITIES BLOCK,* 40-MINUTE PERIODS

Period	Physical Education	Math	Foreign Language	Shop-Home Economics
1		A	CB*	
2	AB	C		Once weekly during
3	AB	D		AB Physical Education
4		B	AD	block.

* During Module 1, Group D, and during Module 4, Group C, appear unaccounted for; in a local scheduling situation they may be assigned to a third area, i.e., Typing.

ALTERNATE DAYS

Period	Physical Education	Math	Foreign Language	Shop-Home Economics
1		C	AD	
2	CD	A		Once weekly during
3	CD	B		CD Physical Education
4		D	BC	block.

Release of academic discipline teachers for purposes of remedial or enrichment assignments can also be accomplished through coverage provided by occasional group guidance classes. The chapter dealing with guidance leads specifically with this concept.

Remedial groups should be scheduled according to certain generally accepted principles:

EXAMPLE 1 – TABLE 13:

SEQUENTIAL BLOCK USING THE TABLE 13 FORMAT

Time	Period	6 Physical Education	6 Math	6 Foreign Language	7 Physical Education	7 Math	7 Foreign Language	8 Physical Education	8 Math	8 Foreign Language
8:20	1		A	CB						
9:00	2	AB	C							
9:40	3	AB	D			A	CB			
10:20	4		B	AD	AB	C				
11:00	5	LUNCH			AB	D				
11:40	6	HUMANITIES				B	AD			
12:20	7	HUMANITIES			LUNCH			LUNCH		
1:00	8	HUMANITIES						AB	A, C	CB
1:40	9	HUMANITIES						AB	D	
2:20–2:50	10	HUMANITIES							B	AD

TABLE 14

A VARIATION ON THE MASTER SCHEDULE,
INCORPORATING PERSONAL DEVELOPMENT
ON A GRADE-LEVEL BASIS

Time	Module	6	7	8
8:15	1			
8:40	2		HUMANITIES	SEQUENTIAL
9:05	3	HUMANITIES		and
9:30	4			PERSONAL
9:55	5		PERSONAL DEVELOP-MENT	DEVELOP-MENT
10:20	6		and	
10:45	7			HUMANITIES
11:10	8		SEQUENTIAL	
11:35	9	LUNCH		
12:00	10	PERSONAL DEVOPMENT		LUNCH
12:25	11	and	LUNCH	
12:50	12	SEQUENTIAL		
1:15	13			
1:40	14		HUMANITIES	HUMANITIES
2:05	15			

1. They should support and be coordinated with the regular program. Whenever possible, materials should relate or be similar to those being covered in regular classes.
2. If students are taken from the humanities area, remedial work should be temporary, or on a basis of rotation

EXAMPLE 1 - TABLE 14:

AN EXAMPLE OF THE 8TH GRADE SEQUENTIAL
TEACHING BLOCK ACCORDING TO
THE TABLE 14 SCHEDULE

Module	Physical Education	Music	Art	Home Economics Shop	Foreign Language
1	AB				CD
2		C		D	
3					
4			C	D	AB
5					
6	P E R S O N A L D E V E L O P M E N T				

through various disciplines. Regular absence from one discipline only creates new weaknesses.

3. The remedial group can easily develop into a "dumping ground" or tracking situation. Regulations or guidelines should be developed regarding proportionate amounts of time any student can be allowed to remain here.

4. Remedial work can be assigned in units. In general, this area is an ongoing class which is quite structured. Enrichment activities, on the other hand, are more terminal, with work administered more independently. For example, a social studies teacher may involve the art teacher for a short period, developing an art-social studies unit with a small enrichment group. Here the teacher acts more as a guide, perhaps referring small groups to the library or other facility. The remedial situation demands constant supervision and assistance by the teacher-in-charge.

5. The remedial group operating during the humanities block can involve both lower level (grammar) and high level (research) skills.

TABLE 15

A MASTER SCHEDULE WHICH IS PARTIALLY
NON-GRADED (40-MINUTE PERIODS)

Period	6	7	8	
1				
2	SEQUENTIAL	HUMANITIES	NON-GRADED	
3				
4	HUMANITIES		Math 7, 8	SEQUENTIAL
5	LUNCH	HUMANITIES 7	Math 7, 8	SEQUENTIAL
6		LUNCH	Alg. 8	
7	HUMANITIES	SEQUENTIAL	Math 7	LUNCH
8			Math 7, 8	HUMANITIES 8
9				

6. The remedial math class can involve general skills development or can take on the function of a permanent small instruction group. The only danger here is the tendency to track a child through homogeneous grouping. The enrichment math group can involve a brief exposure to one or two unusual areas of interest, i.e., computers, electronics.

7. Exploratory-enrichment programs can be scheduled from time to time. Outside speakers, artists, industrial exhibits, group guidance programs, or other guests can be made available for one or more days. Cited in Table 16 is an example of a week-long exploratory-enrichment program scheduled for a humanities block involving four disciplines:

8. Many schools have developed skills-centers which are coordinated with various disciplines. These can be staffed by full-time personnel, paraprofessionals, or rotating teacher-assignment. For example, a math center could involve

TABLE 16

A WEEK-LONG HUMANITIES BLOCK INVOLVING
AN ADDED EXPLORATORY-ENRICHMENT
PERIOD   (ROTATING)

Period		Mon.	Tues.	Wed	Thurs.	Fri.
1	9:00	Exp.(4)	Exp.(1)	Exp.(2)	Exp.(1)	Exp.(4)
2	9:40	1	4	3	2	1
3	10:20	2	1	4	3	2
4	11:00	3	2	1	4	3

children from study-hall situations or those directed from
regular math classes for brief periods. The danger of excessive referral to study centers must be controlled through
appropriate referral precedures and administration.

"Schools without walls,' i.e., Harlem Prep, Philadelphia's
Parkway Academy, have led the way toward flexible movement into enrichment situations or class reorganizations which
lead toward more realistic fulfillment of abilities and needs.

INDEPENDENT STUDY AND CONTRACTS

The merits of these techniques have been discussed in Chapter II. Scheduling poses no great problem other than a need for
student accountability and the necessity for the teacher to follow
closely the student's progress.

Many students view contracts as busy work, often wasting
time and completing the materials at the last moment. It is
necessary, in both areas of independent study and individual
contracts, for the teacher to collect materials or evaluate them
at definite and constant intervals. Given proper organization,
and good sequencing of materials, both of these techniques can
provide invaluable help toward the development of good study
habits and research techniques.

SUMMARY

The authors have reviewed various principles which might be considered in the process of scheduling interdisciplinary programs. The methods of implementing some of the techniques presented in previous chapters were discussed and described through a variety of examples.

six

The role of the teacher in
interdisciplinary programs:
a new profile

The promise of the interdisciplinary program. The interdisciplinary program in the middle school opens new avenues for reaching and "turning on" all pupils and, as it extends a true new curriculum, responds to their needs. Yet of great importance is the fact that the response to these realities must be accomplished in the light of altered professional attitudes. Interdisciplinary teaming, modular scheduling, diagnosis of individual learning difficulties, and other approaches will simply be facades if they are introduced without an accompanying change of attitudes on the part of the staff. It is quite clear to many educators, for example, that modular scheduling can be just as rigid as any traditional schedule. The change to an interdisciplinary program in the middle school, therefore, needs to reflect a change in substance and not just in form. Fortunately, there is enormous potential resident in the middle school concept, for in this idea lies the opportunity to evolve authentically new and rich attitudes about children and about learning. To accomplish this task means to carry out an examination of time-honored assumptions which are held about pupils and how they learn and the milieu in which they live.

A system of schooling which has not changed fundamentally for decades will never really be altered unless those responsible for the conduct of the schools are willing to open themselves up and question some of the conventional wisdom. As this is done, educators need to be ready to accept the new roles for schools, for teachers, and indeed for children. Educators can wait for these new roles to evolve, or they can take an active role in causing them to come about. There are two ways to get to the top of an oak tree: one is to sit on an acorn and wait until it grows and the other is to run up to the tree and climb one hand over the other. Schoolmen might be well advised to do the latter. The promise of the middle school and its interdisciplinary program lies in the opportunities to bring about change.

This instructional pattern is quite typical of many classrooms and accompanies pupils throughout their educational experience from youth to adulthood. There is little wonder, then, that many feel they have no place in the learning environment since they have been set up as passive recipients of data rather than as co-participants in the learning process. It should be no surprise to the perceptive person that pupils in an age of openness and frankness should raise some impolite questions. This feeling is captured by the sensitive expression of a youngster in a letter to her principal about school:

> Students are frustrated and disappointed by an antiquated system that emphasizes discipline, conformity, and marks, especially marks, instead of learning. This school relies on fear, fear of failure, of suspension, of being laughed at, of not getting into a good college. It relies on the intolerable pressure to get grades. . . . In the rush for the mighty mark, learning is lost and school becomes a matter of cramming before the test, of memorizing what the teacher says, spitting it out on the test, of forgetting your ideals, your dreams, your opinions, and conformity and doing the drudgery and busy work dutifully, every day. . . .

What, then, should the interdisciplinary program in the middle school be able to accomplish? The answer, to the authors, is in the moral of a tale of three "wise men" and a simpleton:

While traveling together, this group chanced upon a pile of bones beside the road.

"I can make this pile of bones take shape," said the first wise man.

He uttered some magic and the pile assumed a form.

"I can make the form take on flesh and blood," said the second wise man

He offered his magic and further altered the form.

"My magic can bring the flesh and blood to life," said the third wise man.

"But that is the form of a tiger," said the simpleton. "We should be careful."

"Begone, imbecile!" the wise men shouted, and as the simpleton ran off, the third wise man began his magic.

And sure enough, the tiger came to life and ate up the three wise men.

This tale illustrates the difference between "know-how" and "know-whether." Clearly, we need to build into our educational activities opportunities for pupils to develop the capacity to feel and to question. Pupils need to be guided in the development of a sense of priorities in their lives which reflect a balance between possession of quantities of data (know-how) and a sense of human responsibility and accountability in the course of human interaction (know-whether). Education has been effective in developing the know-how capacity on the part of its charges to perform various tasks such as building this type of political structure and that type of military hardware, etc. But perpaps it has not been as effective in dealing with the capacity of its charges to make the right decisions about the application of its know-how.

Indeed the focus of education historically has been the accumulation of information in encyclopaedic fashion. Education was conceived as an instrument to achieve things. But in addition to the accumulation of information there has to be a focus on the affective areas of learning. The interdisciplinary program in the middle school needs to give pupils the chance to develop know-whether. To do this requires giving pupils and teachers new roles. School must be a game of life where youngsters can try out new ideas, new things and, most importantly, to try out themselves.

We might liken the process of schooling to flight training. If those who train future pilots do an effective job, the trainee may become a successful pilot and thus lessen his chances of failure on the job. This is due to the fact that the trainee had an opportunity to try out a flying machine in a simulated environment and made all his mistakes there. But if his training were not effective, if he did not have a chance to make enough mistakes in the simulated environment, either because the trainers were not understanding enough to allow for mistakes or if they forgot the importance of making mistakes in training, or if perhaps the simulated environment itself were not an accurate enough replica of the actual airplane in which they would eventually fly, then they would not have a very good chance of survival in the real situation. Similarly, in order to educate pupils now for the future, we must use the appropiate tools and attitudes.

Some assumptions questioned. A number of aspects of our system of education which deal with instruction and curriculum need to be examined if an altered approach to teaching-learning is to be realized. Our system of education rests firmly on some of these assumptions:

1. The progression of subjects from the lower grades to the higher grades in the school ladder provides an appropriate sequence for learning.
2. The amount of work to be accomplished in a given school year can be defined precisely and rigidly organized for instruction in any grade.
3. All students in a given class and grade can learn at the same rate.
4. The mastery of a body of knowledge will provide the studdent with the necessary intellectual, social and emotional skills necessary to be accounted as learned.
4. Teacher-centered instructional practices lead to more effective learning outcomes than pupil-centered techniques.
6. Learning takes place better in large groups than in small groups.
7. School is the best place for education to take place.

The traditional teaching role. A decade ago, and indeed in many schools today, if one were to slip in on a number of classrooms in the middle grades, and hover for awhile as Marley's ghost did, one would find a rather consistent pattern of instruction. It would appear much like this: At the opening of the period the teacher would settle the class down, take attendance, and then discuss the previous night's homework. He would proceed to decide on the task at hand for the day and set up the parameters and guidelines to be followed. Next, he would tell the students to open their textbook and he would introduce the new topic and lead the students in a question-and-answer period. Typically he would entertain one question at a time and perhaps call the questioning to a halt when he realized that the 45-minute period was coming to a close. While answering questions he might take the time to rephrase some students' answers and suggest that more attention be paid to the textbook.   At the close of the period he would give the homework assignment and point the way to the next step in their studies.

In the above characterization of a classroom lesson a number of teaching operations are apparent.   For example, the teacher determines what will be taught, the bounds within which he should stay, and the materials and books which will be used. Moreover, he leads the questioning, provides the majority of the information which the students receive during the class, and determines the direction the class will take in the study.   This procedure evidences a lack of confidence in the ability and resourcefulness of pupils, denies the possibility of the great excitement and interest that may be resident in the subject matter; it denies the existence of a variety of creative alternative methods; and implants the idea that the accumulation of data is the essence of being accounted learned.

The new role of the teacher. It is apparent that the new role of the teacher must move beyond that of a provider of information to new perceptions.   An honest challenge of the time-honored assumptions about teaching-learning can bring educators to a substantive new teacher profile. In the following discussion, a modern conception of the role of the teacher will be contrasted with a traditional view. The traditional category (the Know-how Process) outlines a process which places emphasis on know-how and assumes an unquestioned transfer from know-how to actual performance.   The modern view, on the other hand, focuses on the know-whether process while it integrates the process of know-how.

In the know-how process, effective teaching requires that one

- have a mastery or at least a proficiency in a body of subject matter
- know the principles of child growth and development
- know the various theories of learning
- know how to write unit and lesson plans
- know about the different methods and materials for teaching
- know the place and the implications of education in the social order

In the know-whether process, effective teaching requires that one

- have the ability to diagnose learning uniquenesses and difficulties
- have the ability to bring to bear unique and creative approaches to deal with individuals
- have the ability to bring out of children the capacity to solve problems in a way which reflects the teacher's model
- show behavior characterized as non-threatening, secure, sensitive, open to humor.

Given the modern view, what might a professional attitude look like in a classroom? How would we expect a teacher to behave with pupils?

In the role characterized by know-whether, the important assumption is that the source of a teacher's strength is not rooted in techniques and gadgets, but in the character of his being and the style of his mind. Within this educational milieu, teacher-pupil interaction is decidedly open. There is mutual involvement, participation, and planning. The decision as to how to approach a learning problem will be cooperatively determined with the teacher providing a helping hand using his experiences and maturity. Learning via the integration of disciplines will be conducted in ways directly related to the interests and needs of pupils, thus making the question of transfer of training academic. The criteria for appraising learning outcomes will focus on the solution of actual learning situations rather than on the accumulation of data. In this way effective teaching does not require that large quantities of information have been consumed. Instead, effective instruction involves exercising or using behavior. Whatever know-how or knowledge that one may acquire on an intellectual level should be considered latent or potential until it is translated into action or skill. And the quality and nature of this transfer is conditioned by the question pupils raise as they develop the capacity for know-whether. The total instructional program needs to key in on developing this attitude of openness and sensitivity on the part of pupils. Indeed the model the teacher uses will be the example taken by the pupil in building this know-whether. Thus, the essential element a teacher should bring to bear on a situation is the force of himself as a person rather than some intellectual abstractions.

Effective teaching. A fine illustration of effective teaching which employs such characteristics as teacher participation with pupils and the encouragement of pupil decision-making can be seen in the following lesson developed for a sixth grade group dealing with the interdisciplinary theme, "Discovering Who I Am":

Aim: Develop the use of imagination in writing.

Activities.

1. Develop an imaginary creature using descriptive words.

2. Since the object of the lesson is to use the imagination, the creature does not have to be based on what the pupil thinks a creature *ought* to look like. Instead the pupil should be encouraged to let his imagination be free.

3. A list of possible adjectives could be put on the board for pupils to use if they wish.

4. Another alternative would be to have the pupils draw the creature first, and then have them describe the creature; or they may work on the teacher's creature (Figure 6-1).

5. Read two short paragraphs to the group. One terse and to the point; the other will employ description (ask pupils to suggest the sources).

6. Give the pupils the chance to point out the effectiveness of description.

7. Discuss the assignment. Help them tie together the information which has been discussed.

8. List their ideas in their chronicle book

9. Help them select and organize the ideas and images they are going to use.

10. Finalize the creature by writing a descriptive paragraph about it.

11. Open for pupils' ideas or suggestions.

The Homung

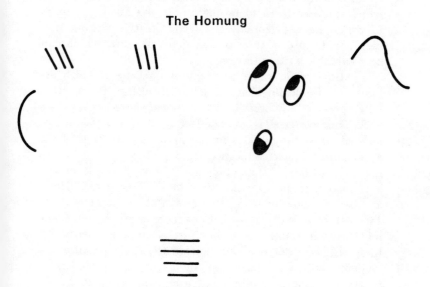

Figure 6-1.

Complete the picture of the "homung" (Figure 6-1). After you have completed the picture of the imaginary animal, write an accurate description of the "homung." Reread your description and see if it is a detailed picture of the cartoon you completed.[1]

Note in the plan below how the teacher is willing to allow eighth graders to be able to raise questions about themselves within the context of a lesson. Using history and literature, the teacher is giving students the opportunities to develop writing skills while they are having the chance to develop the human skills of decision-making and human interaction:

Theme: Discovering Who I Am

Aim: To allow pupils to record feelings they have.

---

[1] Provided by Maureen Shanley, Helen Keller Middle School, Easton, Connecticut.

Activities:

Early adolescents often think that their feelings are unique, for every day they are faced with new and growing personal problems. Creative writing could become a vehicle to vent these intense emotions. It can be a vehicle from which one can learn to be more objective about problems in which he is personally involved. Creative writing enables one to use a third-person point of view, which can be a valuable writing technique.

1. Mimeograph some poems and quotations which exhibit intense feelings about love, friendship, peace, war, hate, greed, or any other basic emotional subject.

2. This exercise is most effective if it can be implemented when the class is in the midst of a turmoil about a particular subject. One perpetual problem is the "ranking out" situation. If an epidemic of ranking people breaks out, then it is an appropos time to use this lesson. There are two reasons for using this lesson at an apropos time. First, creative writing tends to be more original and meaningful when emotion can be injected into it. Secondly, there will be a lot of discussion on the topic because the students will feel personally involved. More important, however, is the possibility that a student will find an alternative answer to a personal problem.

3. Read poems from contemporary poets, who deal with pertinent problems, and historical quotes, which relate to the topic at hand.

4. Discuss each poem and quote separately, and then discuss them as they relate to a single topic. Kahil Gibran's *The Prophet* and Charles Schultz's *Charlie Brown* could produce some interesting comparisons and contrasts on the topic of "What is friendship"? A significant historical quote could be John F. Kennedy's "Ask not what your country can do for you. Ask what you can do for your country."

Assignment:

At home where all is quiet, choose a topic which represents a problem. First, write a paragraph stating your problem. Second, write a paragraph discussing the ramifications of your problem. Third, write a final paragraph which suggests one or more possible solutions to the problem.[2]

---

[2] *Ibid.*

FOCUSING ON THE INDIVIDUAL

The individual pupil. The middle school is an appropriate place in the education of children for them to consider ideas in terms of interrelationships. Their natural desire for inquiry can be coupled with what is a rather sophisticated and impressive fund of learned experiences and a reservoir of information. They often possess sufficient independent skills to enable individual inquiry, and there is a freedom and variety of experiences possible, providing the opportunity for scholarly inquiry. They can pursue learning from relative areas of strength. But, schools often highlight a child's weaknesses (we all have them) and neglect his strengths and as a consequence may do devastating damage. The focus upon the individual then is a major factor in the thrust of interdisciplinary programs in the middle school.

The middle school child, moreover, is involved in a crucial phase of personality development: the development of the self-concept. This occurs at the same time the child identifies with adults and his contemporaries. Also success and failure have an important impact on the self-concept. This self-concept is the view one has of himself and one uses it to measure the world.

Clearly, every effort must be directed toward the development of a healthy and accurate perception of one's self. Therefore, we must provide opportunities in interdisciplinary programs for those personal successes which contribute to the process of fulfilling the potential of pupils. This is referred to by Maslow as the process of self-actualization. It has always been part of the rationale of good teaching and successful human relationships. Interdisciplinary programs in the middle school hold the promise of facilitating the development of healthy self-perceptions.

The positive atmosphere. Focusing on the individual suggests a host of ideas about good teaching within the context of an altered teaching role, as discussed earlier. Instruction in the interdisciplinary program, it was indicated, must achieve a balance between know-how and know-whether. This, in turn, will foster the creation of healthy self-perceptions on the part of pupils. It should be noted that the development of self-perceptions and the creation of positive school environments should not be thought of as separate processes. As a chemical change, one cannot create a compound until the necessary elements are brought together. Likewise, effective learning outcomes cannot be realized without the existence of a positive school atmosphere. This means that the attention of educators should not be confined to such matters as gum chewing or the wearing of jeans. Also, "traditional forms of punishment such as detention and suspension must be replaced, where possible, with a more personalized approach to the problem."[3] More creative, sensible, and humane ways need to be used. Then, perhaps, we may get away from some of the barriers to learning. For example, that aspect of education that is probably the most threatening to students is the setting which conjures up the idea of desks in neat rows facing the front of the room and the front of the teacher's desk. Altering this arrangement is a simple step in creating a good learning climate.

What is a good learning climate in the middle school? In general, building trust, creating informality, constructing relationships of cooperation rather than of competition, and utilizing teachers and pupils as important learning resources are some of the components. Thus, the teacher's role might be thought of in two broad categories: (1) a creator of a warm, empathic and collaborative relationship with the pupils, and (2) a procedural guide and resource. In this context, then, consider some conditions necessary for creating a climate for learning:

1. *Class atmosphere must be warm, friendly and free from threat.* Whenever a pupil feels rejected by teachers or by peers, or senses that any action or comment of his is met by only cold appraisal, his anxiety about himself and how he is getting along with others becomes a major concern. When this happens, the pupil has little enthusiasm or energy left for dealing with problems of learning.

2. *Experimenting and exploring should be encouraged.* While it is important that the classroom provide a warm, emotional climate, this should not become overprotective. Pupils should have opportunities for experimentation, for venturing into the unknown. This, of course, means protection from ridicule in case mistakes are made during the process of experimentation.

3. *The pupil must gradually become independent of the teacher.* It is entirely possible the pupil will become overly

---

[3]Robert J. McCarthy, "Minimizing Discipline Problems by Humanizing the Schools," *Middle School/Junior High Principals Service,* Croft Educational Services, Inc., August, 1970.

dependent upon the teacher. For example, the pupil might work hard in math in order to receive praise from the teacher and his peers but never carry this information home to solve his everyday problems. He might do well with class support in the classroom, but continually have problems in his activities outside of class. However, for effective learning to take place, and to avoid extreme independence or indifference, a continuing and interdependent relationship of mutual trust must exist between the teacher and individual pupils. Such a relationship may prevent social and educational failure.

4. Finally, for effective learning to take place, *there must be effective, three-way communication* — from teacher to pupil, from pupil to teacher, and from pupil to pupil.[4]

Conditions for a good learning situation do not just happen. Sometimes a teacher, sincerely desiring a good climate for learning, mistakenly assumes that it automatically exists. Teachers, for example, repeatedly tell pupils, "I am here to help you. Tell me any problems you might have. We want a situation that is conducive to learning." At the same time, the atmosphere may be cold and forbidding for the pupil to say honestly and freely, "You talk too fast and use words I don't understand."

Communication with pupils. We know that learning is a complex process and has been the subject of research and debate for years. Most agree, however, that learning is defined as a change in behavior and that it takes place as a result of certain types of input. Since learning does not take place in a vacuum — at least the learning we are concerned with in school — and is done principally within the context of the interpersonal relationship between the learner and the one providing the motivation for learning, the nature of the relationship between the teacher and the pupil needs to be reexamined.

Very often when teachers and pupils, and indeed others talk to each other, they really do not listen. As one is presenting a point of view he may not be cognizant of the effect he is having on the recipient. The milieu in which communication is established, the existing attitudes, and the resultant behavior should become serious areas of examination to be undertaken by educators interested in making programs more responsive to young-

---

[4]Adapted from "Climate Setting," by Edward C. Keane, Housatonic Community College, Stratford, Conn. (Unpublished.)

sters. Once an awareness of other people is developed, communications can take place.

Teachers are frequently unaware of the effect their position about one thing or another will have upon pupils. These attitudes are projected on both a verbal and a non-verbal level and indeed can be conscious or subconscious. As the teacher's attitude about pupils develops, it will have an effect on the expectations he will have for them. For example, a teacher may project to pupils that they are not worthy of his attention, or, on the other hand, he may overcompensate by doing too much for them, as is the case of excessive lecturing. This type of communication, carried out with the best of intentions, might have deleterious effects upon the self-image of pupils. Obviously, then, it is imperative that teachers be aware of the effect their attitudes can have on teacher-pupil relationships. Functioning in an interdisciplinary program in the middle school, then, requires that teachers have a high degree of awareness and sensitivity.

Diagnosis. The process of diagnosis should not be alien to the teaching process if teaching is conceived as a process to help fulfill the individual child. Therefore, in order to achieve this goal, it is important that the teacher have information and insight about the learner so that he can begin to assist him. Perhaps one of the most widespread agreements among educators is that children are indeed different in terms of their backgrounds, interests, learning capacities, and so forth. The important thing, however, is that the instructional program truly reflect this view. What this amounts to is making the learning situation responsive to the needs of individual pupils. As Figure 6-2 illustrates, if a teacher begins instruction with a whole class of pupils at a single level of instruction, those who are not at *that* level will feel frustrated.

The notion that pupil involvement in learning activities enhances learning outcomes is also a currency. Given these understandings and the fact that large classes or the existence of groups of any size make it difficult (but not impossible) to respond to individuals, diagnosis of learning needs becomes an essential component of teaching.

The process whereby teachers help pupils identify specific learning needs and help them plan and set up experiences to achieve these may be called diagnostic teaching. Dorris May Lee offers five elements crucial in diagnostic teaching. They are that:

1. Each learner must learn how to establish his own goals and purposes.
2. He must be steadily aware of these goals and purposes.
3. He must devise for himself as well as plan with the teacher ways of achieving each goal as well as ways of recognizing the accomplishment.
4. Within reasonable limits, each student must be self-directing and self-pacing, and free to choose immediate goals, materials and procedures.
5. As far as possible, both teacher and learner must be aware of longer term goals and larger frameworks of concepts to be developed so that these may be used as guides to more immediate steps in teaching and learning.[5]

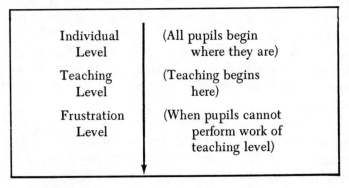

Individual Level	(All pupils begin where they are)
Teaching Level	(Teaching begins here)
Frustration Level	(When pupils cannot perform work of teaching level)

Figure 6-2. Teaching-learning readiness.

Characteristically, diagnostic teaching is a move away from the traditional use of the self-contained group or class as the basic non-changing unit of instruction. The hallmark of diagnostic teaching is flexibility in grouping and in organizing students in learning activities. Here, the teacher is not the sole source of information but, instead, the authentic change agent. In this situation, consistent with interdisciplinary programs in the middle school, the teacher is the provider, the aid, the facilitator. He becomes a co-participator with the pupils in learning and

---

[5]Dorris May Lee in *Teaching and Evaluation as Feedback and Guide* (Washington, D.C.: Association for Supervision and Curriculum Development, 1967), p. 74.

can share in their enthusiasm and in their discovering. Also the teacher has the opportunity to project his own enthusiasm.

This suggests a number of teaching possibilities which would enhance the development of the individual; for example, the flexibility permits the teacher to spend more time with individuals in dealing with their unique needs and assisting them in appraising themselves. But, to be effective, the confidence of the pupil must be won in an atmosphere free from threat and intimidation.

Focus on the slow learner. Innovations in curriculum and instruction can sometimes be viewed, erroneously, as being for the talented or advantaged since the children from slums or those with learning disabilities cannot handle such programs. Apparently some feel that the process of teaching and learning is more effective (or safer and easier) for disadvantaged pupils when carried out in terms of conventional teaching and curriculum arrangements. Program flexibility, independent study and decision making are outside the capabilities of this group, some argue. Yet it is precisely these disadvantaged youngsters or slow learners who desperately need and can profit from interdisciplinary programs.

There can be some exciting possibilities for such youngsters in the middle grades. Indeed, there are a number of interdisciplinary curriculum arrangements that can be employed for slow learners in a middle school. For example, to motivate culturally disadvantaged pupils or slow learners, those who might be described as "in-school dropouts," a more effective use of the unified arts program may be developed. Small groups can learn sixth grade arithmetic in shop or mechanical drawing areas through a program that is specifically designed to coordinate mathematical learning with industrial arts skills. Girls, on the other hand, can do the same type of thing in home economics by computing single proportions in recipes and calculating percentage of waste.

It must be emphasized that this experience must extend beyond the trivia of many conventional educational programs. Total involvement and follow-through is needed by whichever vehicle the teacher as well as the pupil finds that best educates. For example, if a pupil interested in Afro-American history can relate this to a study of Western culture, he should at some time be given the opportunity to do so. The teacher-team, apprised of the pupil's weakness, say in written expression, can skew its expectations accordingly, but build it around an Afro-American history experience.

The assignment of tasks into small group experiences can saturate a youngster in areas needing strengthening under the watchful eye of one or more of the teachers. Likewise, large-group instruction can free some members of the team, enabling them to work independently with either small groups or with individual gifted as well as the culturally disadvantaged or slow learners.

There is no absence of structure here, nor is it a laissez-faire atmosphere of children running around with individual projects. Structure and planning are there and direction must be established by the teachers. However, fulfillment of this direction must occur through the pupil's individual needs and interests. Indeed, teachers should show as much interest in how a specific child is learning as in what he might have learned.

SUMMARY

In this chapter a new profile of the teacher was examined in the context of the interdisciplinary program. The position suggested was that the teacher be a resource and an aid to the pupil in learning, rather than a dictator. The learning climate should be established in relation to a positive attitude on the part of the teacher which can promote self-assessment and professional growth. Inherent in the idea of the interdisciplinary approach and the program which focuses on the individual is the concept of diagnostic teaching. In this way the teaching-learning situation must proceed from an analysis of the learning level of youngsters to a series of prescribed learning activities. This is based on the belief that not all youngsters are at the same level of learning readiness.

seven

Teaching strategies in the interdisciplinary program

In other chapters we discussed the development of realistic interdisciplinary programs for the middle school, the effective use of facilities, building schedules, and ways to interest and involve the staff. Our task in this chapter is to explore some effective approaches in teaching in interdisciplinary programs in the middle school. This will be done in the light of the emerging new roles of the teacher and the pupils. Since the interdisciplinary approach focuses on the fulfillment of the individual pupil, it has significant implications for teaching.

Individualization of instruction. Teaching strategies become the vehicle through which the educational philosophy of the program can be achieved. And the hallmark of interdisciplinary programs in the middle school is their emphasis on an educational and social climate which maximizes the self-fulfillment of the individual child. This goal then can be achieved through the individualization of instruction for all students. Individualizing becomes a teaching technique or strategy to actualize the philosophy of the interdisciplinary approach. At the same time the concept of individualization of instruction offers great promise for education, it also has been badly misused and misunderstood by lay people and educators alike. Danowski has set the picture in order when he set out to define individualized instruction. He established indicators with reference to teacher behavior and pupil behavior which, when applied, could tell whether an instructional situation is individualized or not. The characteristics which describe individualizing and nonindividualizing, as seen below, are helpful in developing individualized teaching strategies.

POLAR CHARACTERISTICS DISTINGUISHING INDIVIDUALIZING FROM NON-INDIVIDUALIZING TEACHING PRACTICES[1]

Observed Behavior in Classrooms of Individualizing Teachers	Observed Behavior in Classrooms of Non-Individualizing Teachers
Teacher Behavior	
Individualizing Pole	*Non-Individualizing Pole*
Objectives	
The teacher pursues multiple objectives, each objective related to a specific pupil or a small group of pupils.	The teacher pursues a single objective applying it without variation to all pupils in the class.
Planning and Preparation	
The teacher's planning and preparation are in terms of individual students.	The teacher's planning and preparation are in terms of some single class norm. (This norm may be the average of the three or four "best" students.)
Communication-Direction	
The teacher communicates with individuals in the class while other individuals of class remain engaged in different activities.	The teacher communicates with all pupils in the entire class at one and the same time (i.e., "out loud"), even when addressing one youngster.

---

[1] Charles E. Danowski, "Individualization of Instruction: A Functional Definition," *Research Bulletin*, Institute of Administrative Research, Teachers College, Columbia University, Vol. 5, No. 2 (February, 1965).

Communication-Message

The teacher uses feedback information from individual pupils as a basis for modifying the message being communicated	The teacher's preselected communication is unmodified by circumstances other than his own objectives, or by variations in its reception by individual pupils

Function

The teacher's function is primarily observation of evidences of learning, or the lack of it, and the motivation and guiding of students to independent learning activity.	The teacher functions primarily as a purveyor of information

Evaluation

The teacher's evaluation of each pupil is based on the latter's individual growth and development	The teacher evaluates the pupils en masse with a predetermined standard as the measure of success.

Pupil Behavior

Objectives

The pupils pursue objectives which they themselves have established.	The pupils pursue objectives which the teacher has established.

Planning and Preparation

The pupil's planning and preparation have been unique in that they are engaged in independent work, study, practice, or demonstration.	The pupil's planning and preparation have been by teacher's direction in that all pupils are engaged in the same activity.

Communication-Direction

The pupils are engaged in small group activity in which discussion is considered a function of learning.	The pupils' participation in class is restricted to asking or answering questions of the teacher.

Communication-Message

The pupils are encouraged to manifest originality, creative productivity, and purposeful divergence.	The pupils are restricted to recitation of predigested material and to conformity

Function

The pupils are active participants in learning activities.	The pupils are passive recipients of knowledge.

Evaluation

The pupil evaluates his own growth and development.	The pupil makes no self-evaluation but accepts teacher's opinion.

Independent study. A very effective method of focusing instruction on the individual is the independent study or task contract. In the model that follows, the pupil and the teacher assume responsibilities in the learning activity:

An agreement entered into between pupil, -------------- and teacher, --------------

I. *Preliminaries*

Before beginning this task the pupil shall have submitted an outline of the task to the teacher.

II. *Nature of the Work*

Briefly describe the task on the back of this contract

III. *Approximate Time Needed*

It is estimated that this task shall require _____weeks to complete.

IV. *Task of the Pupil*

1. The pupil shall meet the preliminaries described above.
2. The student shall meet twice a week with the teacher to seek assistance in the completion of the task (and whenever needed).
3. The pupil shall prepare a report on the findings of his task.

V. *The Role of the Teacher*
1. The teacher shall consult with the pupil regularly and shall offer all appropriate guidance in the preparation of the task.
2. The teacher shall free the student to use any resource materials or equipment.
3. During the task the teacher and pupil shall assess and review the progress.
4. The teacher and the pupil may terminate the task at any time they feel the task has become unnecessary.

VI. *The Role of the Administration*
1. The administration shall permit the pupil to be released from scheduled activities in order to prepare the task and shall make available all facilities.
2. The administration shall hold the pupil responsible for observance of all school rules and regulations during the development of his task.

Pupil	Teacher	Date

Another method for launching an independent study is suggested by the Proposal for Independent Study drafted by the Fox Lane Middle School staff. Note in the items below the emphasis on pupil decision-making:

PROPOSAL FOR INDEPENDENT STUDY[2]

I. My proposal
   A. For my independent study project I would like to:
   B. The goals that I have set for myself in doing this are:
   C. The method of procedure that I plan to follow seems now to be:

II. I choose this particular project because:

III. I want to have the opportunity to pursue this course of study on my own because:

IV. The approximate length of time I think I will need to work is:

---

[2]Provided by Dr. Malcolm Rizzutto, Fox Lane Middle School, Bedford, N.Y. (Mimeographed; 1969.)

V. Special materials, resources, equipment, facilities, or aid I think I will need are:

VI. My preference (if any) for a faculty advisor is:

For an illustration of an invitation to students to undertake independent study, see Appendix V. Here is a good example of how to ease pupils into independent work. Moreover, it is the type of procedure which should be adopted by schools wishing to convert to an interdisciplinary program from a more traditional arrangement.

The individual prescription. Once the diagnosis of educational needs has been made, the task of prescribing instructional follow-up is in order. Moving from the identified instructional level of the pupil to the instructional prescription is a strategy in teaching which requires some skill and, even more, a commitment to the concept of individualizing instruction. Since pupils learn at different rates, the teacher will be faced with different learning prescriptions. It is possible that each pupil could have his own individual prescription, different from the other pupils'. Alternatively, there could be a number of learning modules or study units available where groups can study within a common area.

Let us examine a model of a prescriptive plan based on a process of diagnosis. A pupil entering a learning environment is given a series of diagnostic achievement tests in reading, language arts, and arithmetic in order to determine an educational readiness profile. Establishing a favorable rapport with the pupil is essential when carrying out a diagnosis. If standardized tests are used, or other packaged instruments, it is important that a non-threatening atmosphere be established. To build this atmosphere it is wise to have the tests administered in such a way that the pupils understand the teacher is trying to find out something about the level at which they are. From this, it should be understood, the teacher can tailor the program for the pupil individually. The test should not be thought of by pupils as a device to fail them. Efforts should be made, therefore, to create a "non-test" situation. This can be accomplished by avoiding standardized tests until a positive rapport has been developed. Informal teacher-made inventories, observations and personal interviews can be used instead. The message the teacher really wants to get across to the pupil is that he simply wants to find out where to begin instruction.

When the educational level has been determined, an instructional program can be designed for the pupils which should permit the pupil to develop a sense of self-direction and confidence in himself. Such individualization of instruction, it should be noted, promotes the idea of learning in terms of interdisciplinary themes. In this arrangement, pupils' progress can be monitored periodically by the teachers involved, while at the same time youngsters are encouraged to carry out self-appraisals. As a result they will have a more meaningful approach to what they are learning and hopefully will have the stimulation and motivation to continue to learn.

Learning based on individualized prescriptions will be characterized by activities in which youngsters will find themselves working in small and large groups throughout an instructional program. In this regard, as we shall see later in the discussion on simulations, peer interaction must continue to be fostered. Prescribing individualized programs does not, nor should it mean eliminating group work or contact with peers.

While pursuing a particular interdisciplinary theme such as Aggression, it would be necessary perhaps for pupils to veer off from the major body of study and take a side trip to a skill or remedial unit. This could be based on assessments made cooperatively by the pupils and the teacher as the instructional program progresses. A pupil could remain on the side trip, for example, for a relatively long period of time in order to develop a particular skill in mathematics or in writing and then return to the main area of study to join the others. Another alternative would be for the youngster to leave the larger group periodically for short doses daily, but still spend most of his time in the large-group study. In addition, the pupil may pursue an area of personal interest as an independent study. The flexibility of this scheme allows for multiple alternatives and this indeed is a major strength.

Simulation. The concept of relevance is a principal thread which has permeated our discussions of teaching. To help pupils achieve a balance of know-how and know-whether, it is important that learning activities have relevance and meaning for them. In this sense it is not so much what is taught that suggests relevance, but rather the way in which it is taught. Pupils need to understand why things are important and how the skills they acquire in school may be applied outside of school. Thus, in an effort to motivate children to think about what they are learning and to involve them in the learning activities, techniques of simulation are proposed.

Simulations permit teacher and pupils to build an environment where pupils can play roles which are believable or which may be models of actual roles they may play or must relate to later in life.

Simulation may be defined as a representation of reality in a way which eliminates both the elements of expense and danger for the participant while providing only those components of reality which are necessary for the experience. The representation or model of reality may be of a physical situation or a social situation. In the former, for example, the Link trainer used in World War II to prepare pilots was a model of an actual airplane in flight. An illustration of a model of a social system would be a village of a primitive tribe in which a selected number of social challenges were available for participants to be involved. In this case, pupils could simulate the environment and develop insights into the culture of primitive peoples without running the risk of losing their heads to head-hunters or incurring the travel expense to faraway places.

The structure of this type of activity lends itself well to the individualization of instruction since it creates the proper climate for pupils. And it is this climate for learning, characterized by teacher-pupil openness and co-participation, which is fostered by simulation activities. As a teaching device, simulations have rich potential. They encourage a great deal of involvement of the participants and the players can see the results of their decisions immediately. Moreover, simulations permit players to actually behave rather than to merely verbalize.

A significant advantage of simulation games is the gains made in communicative skills, persuasion and influence-resisting techniques. Simulation seems to be appropriate for all ability levels . . . each child can find his own level of success. In the debriefing session that follows, the class compares outcomes, strategies or consequences of actions which helps to put things into perspective for the individual. Since the concepts and facts replicate life situations, they are more relevant to the student and probably are learned more easily and retained longer.

Applying simulation games with pupils. There is no "best" way to play a simulation game. The situation may vary because pupils and teachers vary. However, two basic types of outcomes are likely to result from playing simulation games: (1) there may be immediate insight or understanding, and (2) there may be follow-up, long-term learnings which occur as pupils continue to study related concepts and topics; that is, pupils may relate experiences they had in the game to a number of different situations which may arise in the future.

In *Generation Gap,* published by Western Publishing Company in New York, which is appropriate for middle school youngsters, a number of learnings may be expected which have both immediate and long-range impacts. Its aim is to develop self-confidence and human relations skills on the part of pupils so that they may be more sensitive to others. In this game, participants have an opportunity to explore the conflicts which exist between superiors and subordinates (parent-child). Parent and a teenager work out problems such as staying out late, working around the house, good grooming, and dating. As the game proceeds and the players learn, several things become apparent: It is possible to develop trust in a relationship even though one party has greater legitimate power; that authority, too, has its difficulties, and exerting power is not the best approach always; and that it is best to communicate on all problems and work toward a compromise.

Generation Gap can be adapted to several types of interdisciplinary themes, such as aggression, the family, communication, etc. It should be noted that the issues or problems need not be confined to conflicts between parent and child. Indeed, in studying various themes a wide variety of role conflicts can be used with their related problems. Some examples are the conflicts which take place between teacher and pupil, pupil and principal, project leader and pupil, etc.

It is really quite easy and fun for youngsters to develop their own model situations and related problems. Commercially produced games such as the one discussed above and others (see Appendix VII for simulations appropriate for the middle grades) can be used to stimulate pupils to be creative. The teacher should also try to build a simulation game and encourage pupil suggestions and alterations. If one follows the basic structure of simulations, as discussed earlier, one can capitalize on the un- limited possibilities. The following problems between a pupil and a teacher illustrate some of this:

Teacher	Pupil
• Your assigned classwork comes first, and you will attend all sessions.	I will not attend sessions if they are not meaningful to me.
• Swearing and vulgarity are not permitted in this group.	Freedom of speech gives me the right to say what I want in school.
• Marks are important in deciding on group place- ment and motivate you to learn, therefore more unit tests.	Marks are demoralizing and force kids to cheat.

Let us consider a further use of simulation. Using the theme Aggression, an interdisciplinary team might build a unit around this theme with the idea of assisting pupils in understanding the significance, past and present, of human aggressiveness in inter- national relations, politics, business and commerce, and inter- personal relationships. In the study, a simulation exercise could be introduced where pupils are given the problem, for example, of working out a compromise urban redevelopment plan which would satisfy rival community factions and governmental agen- cies. In trying to help them develop an understanding of ag- gression, involvement in a game such as *Generation Gap* could help develop the sensitivity and tact needed in interpersonal re- lationships. Out of this activity, the youngsters would have gain- ed experience in writing, researching, thinking, debating, and working together. They would end up with a better understand- ing of themselves, and all in all it would have been an exciting unit.

Team planning. The preparation for instruction needs to be carried out within the context of the interdisciplinary program. Since the interdisciplinary curriculum is based on several fields of study, planning must involve all members of the team so that the interrelationship between the disciplines occurs. Each member of the team is responsible for his own discipline in terms of assisting students in learning the basic concepts and skills for that discipline. But the traditional barriers between the academic disciplines do not go beyond this point. The team presents an interdisciplinary unit based on a broad theme relevant to pupils and, moreover, one which has invited their involvement. How should these themes be selected? In what sequence should they be presented? Who shall be responsible for teaching? The answers to this type of inquiry should emerge in the planning.

To illustrate, take the theme, Aggression. The social studies specialist on the interdisciplinary team would be the likely person to take the lead in developing and presenting this particular theme. Social studies, in fact, would probably be the dominant discipline in the unit. But the concept of aggression is also developed in literature, and would be explored by pupils in composition and debate, and so the English specialist on the team could be satisfied that his discipline was getting fair treatment.

Aggression has its roots in individual and mass psychology — and in biology, according to some authorities — and leading pupils in an exploration of these considerations would be the responsibility of the science specialist. As for the mathematics specialist, he would use his influence to insure that the unit was so structured so to include relevant activities that would lend themselves to the learning of such mathematical skills and concepts as graphing, probability, fractions, percentages, and computation. This could be accomplished in side trip skill sessions or interest and enrichment activities.

The essential idea is that the curriculum themes be meaningful to youngsters and that the learning activities focus on motivating interest and involvement with the theme. Members of the interdisciplinary team will need to carry out continuous planning and monitoring. More than likely, they will be unable to plan very far in advance if the learning activities are to be responsive to pupils. When planning for instruction, "it should not be supposed that all one's intentions will be fulfilled in one class period or module. The design of a lesson plan should not be so rigid as to constrain the teacher to one class or class meeting. The plan presents the avenue; time will take care of itself and may not be the significant factor. Student interest and motivation may draw out a planned learning segment."[3]

The study log. A helpful device for use by members of the interdisciplinary team when planning themes is the Study Log. The following Log illustrates a number of important questions which need to be raised by the team as it focuses on the individual. Such a log is also appropriate for monitoring on-going teaching-learning:

STUDY LOG[4]

Interdisciplinary Theme: _____

1. Content segments specified:
2. What assumptions can we make regarding a pupil's requisite knowledge and skills?
3. What are our specific objectives for pupils in terms of this content?
4. What methods of review will we use?
5. What kinds of experiences and models can we use in reviewing?
6. What motivating experiences and devices can we use to introduce the lesson?
7. What pupil activities can we use to sustain the learning experience?

Lesson plans. The following lesson plans are appropriate for middle school interdisciplinary programs and illustrate some successful activities for focusing on the individual within an interdisciplinary program:

Interdisciplinary Theme: Communication

Aim: Development of the use of colloquial language in creative writing.

A dry, ordinary plot can be revitalized by colloquial speech patterns. Pupils often write stories using formal language patterns because they don't clearly understand the difference between factual and creative writing. For example, if a pupil is trying to create a rough and ready character, then he should employ the language of that type of character rather than the type of language used by his

---

[3]Joseph DeVita, Philip Pumerantz, and Leighton B. Wilklow, *The Effective Middle School* (West Nyack, N.Y.: Parker Publishing Company, 1970), p. 191.

[4]Provided by Dr. Malcolm Rizzutto, Fox Lane Middle School, Bedford, N.Y.

teachers. The emphasis on colloquial speech could produce more realistic or believable characters and stories, as well as a better appreciation of how communication takes on different levels of understanding.

Activities:

Have two basic types of material mimeographed for the pupils. Both writing samples should deal with the same type of information, but one should be very formal in its use of language while the other should employ less formal speech patterns. Mark Twain and Henry James could be used as examples of the two different types of writing. Most children will enjoy Twain's writing more because the colloquial speech patterns which he used appeal to younger people more than the heavy description used in James' writing.

1. Read the two samples.

2. Discuss how, when, and why the technique of colloquial speech could be of use to a writer.

3. Help them to see that colloquial speech patterns are used only when there is dialogue taking place. For example, Mark Twain employed colloquial speech patterns only when the characters were carrying on a dialogue. The rest of the story employed a more formal type of language pattern because most readers would find it too difficult to read an entire book which was not written in the standard American dialect. To further illustrate this point, bring in some novelettes written by people *from* the ghetto *for* people in the ghetto. Most people have great difficulty just trying to get the basic gist of the story.

4. Ask the pupils to recount some incident which has involved them. In their written narrative descriptions, they are to employ both formal and informal language patterns.

Interdisciplinary Theme: Discovering Who I am

Aim: The development of the use of personal experiences as a resource technique in the development of believable characters to be used in creative stories.

When pupils are asked to write compositions, a favorite cry is "I can't think of anything." One of the reasons why some have this problem is because they do not use personal experiences in their writing. It is common knowledge that professional writers rely heavily on personal experience in order to create realistic, believable characters. This can also help the pupil to develop a better understanding of *who* he is and how he relates to others.

Activities:

Have pupils find a picture in a magazine which represents a situation in which they have been involved. For example, suggest a picture of a man who, when he reaches the check-out stand in a supermarket, suddenly realizes that he has forgotten his wallet. This situation could be related from at least three points of view: the cashier, the man himself, or the person standing behind him in line watching all that is taking place.

Have each pupil communicate the experience from both the picture he has chosen, and his own personal experience. (He may choose the vehicle to do this, i.e., a composition, oral report, etc.)

Interdisciplinary Theme: Communications

Aim: Development of the use of dialogue in writing

Youngsters are tuned into T.V. dialogue, but they often have trouble using dialogue in writing. If they could associate a familiar part of their daily environment with the act of writing dialogue, then perhaps it would be easier for them to use dialogue in creative writing. The theme of the dialogue could relate to the historical, scientific, or mathematical area which they are studying.

Activities:

1. Read a play and permit pupils to see that the dialogue in the play is just like a conversation between two or more people.

2. Help them see the need for and the use of stage directions.

3. Ask each pupil to write a script for a puppet play which they may present to the class. The puppet play may be based on any related subject of their choosing. They should be encouraged to choose plays about subjects important to them.

Interdisciplinary Theme: Discovering Who I Am

Aim: Development of depth of ideas.

A pupil often "knows" he dislikes something, but, like adults, he does not always know exactly *why* he dislikes something.

Activities:

Ask the pupil to write down a broad area which he finds troublesome to himself (parents, insults, prejudice, school, or going steady). After he has chosen a subject, then he should think about specific incidents which relate to his chosen subject.

1. Have the pupil head a piece of notebook paper with the broad subject area he has chosen.

2. After he has given some thought to his subject, he should list the reasons why he feels this problem exists.

3. The pupil should then review what he has written and decide if he has *any* form of control over some of the reasons for his problem.

4. He should then choose one of the areas in which he could exhibit some control and write two compositions. One composition should show how he originally acted in the difficult situation, while the second composition should show how he could have reacted if he had given the situation more thought

Interdisciplinary Theme: Man in the Ecological Setting

Aim: The objective is to give the pupil the opportunity to try to use the writing skills which he has been observing while he has been reading novels.

After the pupil has read *Danny Dunne and the Homework Machine* and *The Furious Flycycle,* the teacher could suggest that the pupil might try to write a short story based on a scientific invention which he would like to make. If he has enjoyed one or both of the novels, then he can employ a multitude of writing techniques as well as some scientific concepts which might be fresh in his mind.

Activities:

1. Have the pupil write down a technical problem which he would like to solve.

2. Ask the pupil to think of different ways to solve the problem. The solutions should be logical in the sense that if one tried to put the invention together it might prove to be mechanically feasible. The main objective is to try to approach an old problem from a new point of view.

3. Have the pupil make a list of the details he wants to use in his story.

After ne has selected a solution to his problem, he can

begin to write his rough draft. Originality, as well as paragraph structure, is an important aspect of this writing exercise.

SUMMARY

This chapter considered independent study plans, and other individualized techniques were explored in an effort to provide alternative ways to free pupils to learn. And for an additional teaching tool, simulation games were proposed. If pupils can play the roles of various personalities in an imitated situation, it can be effective in developing the conceptual and human relations skills which are important to the creation of a favorable balance between know-how and know-whether.

Finally the development of lesson plans which focus on the individual in an interdisciplinary program were suggested as appropriate for a number of curriculum themes.

eight

Guidance in
interdisciplinary programs

The authors will discuss the Pupil Personnel Program and its importance in the middle school. The appraisal of the individual student's potential, skills and interests is of paramount importance in any school which has as its central thrust the maximum development of the individual. The special nature of the inter-disciplinary program, with its emphasis upon individualization in academic and personal development areas, dictates the necess-ity for good pupil evaluation and guidance.

The contribution of the guidance counselor, psychologist and other pupil personnel workers has long been accepted as a valid and important part of the educational program. Additionally, in creased importance has been rendered these areas as a result of the pressures of our dynamic, mobile and complex society.

Our discussions thus far should have indicated those changed or increased responsibilities and demands placed upon the in-dividual teacher as a result of interdisciplinary programming.

We have seen one essential change in the teacher's role: his more dynamic involvement in curriculum and grouping. Does this similarly affect the guidance counselor or other members of the pupil personnel team? Do the functions and responsibilities of teachers, counselors, and administrators overlap more than they do in the traditional program? What are these functions? Can a more effective job be done in meeting individual needs? These questions will be considered here in a practical way through a discussion of the pupil personnel program, its rationale and structure.

THE NEED FOR GUIDANCE

In the traditional program, guidance evolved as a separate student-personnel function with the specific responsibility improving pupil behavior through the prevention of problems, improving individual adjustment and better understanding the individual.[1] While these continue to be major responsibilities, the dynamic middle school program has provided many opportunities for closer counselor and teacher involvement with students. The guidance function can no longer be identified as being conceived almost exclusively with those students having more serious problems. It has become a visible part of the total educational program.

Transescent youngsters have always been faced with a multitude of social, physical, emotional and general maturational needs. However, the contemporary middle school youth is additionally confronted with a tumultuous society undergoing major changes in traditions as values. The transescent period is often a time where rejection of parental dependency occurs, when new peer values and identification with certain adults receive greater priority. The teacher and counselor, through their availability at the interpersonal level, can help youngsters during this crucial period of development. Current thinking among many educators involved with middle school youth emphasizes that the guidance function must become an active part of the instructional

---

[1] D. G. Mortensen and A. M. Schmuller, *Guidance in Today's Schools* (New York: John Wiley & Sons, 1959), pp. 10-12.

program. The teacher must assume more responsibility for guidance. Conversely, the counselor must become more involved in curriculum, and in its relationships for each student.

In the interdisciplinary program, there occurs a teacher shift from subject orientation to a focus upon the student. By the same token, we recommend that the counselor modify his therapy-oriented role to include a function as mental-health leader among teachers. The teacher, while working within the restrictions of his teaching responsibilities and the limitations of his training in guidance, can still provide a second-echelon guidance role. Consequently, the counselor, while properly serving as a member of the Pupil Personnel Team, broadens his involvement by becoming a participant on the *Teacher-Counselor-Team.*

THE TEACHER-COUNSELOR TEAM

The teacher. The participation of teachers in certain guidance functions is essential. The teacher is often the first to detect difficulties and make referrals for counseling or other personnel services. He is in a position to observe the child in the day-to-day situation. In addition, he views the child in a peer situation, an experience often unavailable to the counselor. The type of relationship based upon mutual cooperation between teacher and pupil personnel specialist is not new, but the more flexible school atmosphere improves opportunities for more effective collaboration. Neither party needs to abdicate his function to the other any more than the social studies specialist or the art teacher does when cooperating mutually toward more effective instruction. It must be emphasized that only certain areas of guidance are necessarily involved here, for the authors do not consider, at this point, those special skills and competencies requiring special training. Test interpretation, appraisal of certain psychological data, counseling on a regular and personal level, and other factors must, by their nature, be regarded as guidance or pupil personnel functions. These will be considered in greater detail when defining the specific duties of teachers and pupil personnel specialists.

Enumerated below are those specific areas where the teacher can contribute to the personal and emotional well-being of the student, hopefully in cooperation with teacher colleagues or pupil personnel specialists.

1. He should be cognizant of the major functions of guidance, and the resources available to him through the pupil personnel staff. The teacher's immediate liaison is usually with the guidance counselor.

2. He should assist the child in the development of a realistic self-concept.

3. He should be aware of the basic principles of guidance, counseling, and psychology, at least being aware of the major indicators of personality malfunction, so that referral might be made at the appropriate time. He must understand the non-directive nature of guidance and its implication that young people must learn to make wise decisions for themselves.

4. He must also realize that, in addition to instruction and educational experiences, we assist the student on a personal level by helping him (a) to make wise decisions and choices, (b) to recognize, strengthen and develop his abilities, (c) to face problems he will encounter in and out of school, and (d) to strengthen his power to use his own abilities.

5. As a member of a teacher-team, he should assist each child toward the experiencing of personal successes whenever possible. He might encourage a colleague to contribute his more profound skills at a strategic time. The counselor or psychologist might enlist the combined resources of the team, either to observe a student's behavior or to develop a planned program of remediation or enrichment. He encourages student independence and helps with grouping.

6. He often initiates important information for the cumulative record and may be first to identify the specific academic or personal area needing additional support. He keeps in contact with other specialists involved in the particular situation, and follows through.

7. He makes distinction between disciplinary referrals (to administration) and appropriate referrals to guidance.

8. The teacher is often the first to become aware of a child's personal, home or peer problems.

9. The teacher realizes that the ultimate coordination and responsibility for the pupil personnel needs of the student rest in the counselor's hands. Referrals to other professionals must be made through the counselor. Parental contact involving guidance implications should be communicated to the counselor.

The teacher may assume more formal, second-echelon pupil personnel functions in school systems where there is a shortage of trained personnel. It is again emphasized that the function should necessarily be limited to the competencies enjoyed by the "teacher-counselor." Proponents of the nondirective, client-centered approach might argue that the entire teacher-counselor concept is in itself a contradiction, for the counselor cannot wear two hats. They would probably argue that the basis for a good relationship implies a nondirective image on the part of the counselor. The teacher, by his directive role on one hand, would be unable to effectively fulfill the counselor role. This argument could be accurate in the cases of some children; however, the middle school child will often relate to a teacher, particularly on a superficial level. There has been significant success with this approach at the middle school level, through the employment of the Teacher-Counselor approach. This arrangement makes it possible for children to have a regularly assigned period in which group activities can be carried on, but where they might be under the supervision of a teacher who acts as their first-line counselor. The children can refer a problem either to the regularly assigned teacher or to a member of the teacher team. This might involve referral to the guidance counselor, or might be handled quite simply at this level. The home-base, teacher-counselor becomes either a referral agent or one who handles many problems individually and in small groups. Schools employing modular or interdisciplinary-block scheduling can schedule daily home-base periods. The traditional home room period can also be extended for this approach.

The teacher-counselor approach can fulfill an important function, but it is supplementary in nature and supports a centralized guidance organization.

The teacher relates to certain pupil personnel activities in concert with members of the pupil personnel staff.

The guidance counselor. The responsibilities of the counselor are rather broad and often involve a one-to-one relationship with the student. The counselor is involved in individual appraisal through testing or personal contact. It is essential that he continually remain apprised of the students' school performance, particularly through contact with teachers and as a firsthand observer.

Students should have an opportunity to develop insights and to solve problems as a result of the group or individual counseling relationship provided by the counselor.

Information sharing is another task performed with the student, parent and teacher. This usually is essential for academic planning and for providing alternatives for decision-making. The counselor in the contemporary school setting can make more effective use of test data than has generally been the case in the past. This includes increased sharing and interpretation of test data with the parent and the student. The student should certainly be aware of his performance in areas of achievement testing, and can profit from a realistic appraisal of specific aptitudes. Test publishers have developed many effective devices which aid in the presentation and interpretation of test data. Profile charts are available for most tests, and can be valuable tools in the hands of the effective counselor.

Educators and parents are aware of the difficult maturational changes experienced by transescent youth. Personality development and physical growth create problems for young people and require counselor support. Continued evaluation and follow-up must seek to insure that manifestations of these do not needlessly deprive children of appropriate opportunities to develop their potential.

In the interdisciplinary situation the counselor must become more involved in curriculum and adjust programs in accordance with the team effort. He works closely with the head teacher or team members.

He is often the liaison between the teacher and the pupil personnel staff and collects pertinent information for case conferences or referrals.

The pupil personnel team. We will briefly refer to the Pupil Personnel Team, since this group provides specialized services within the middle school. With the exception of the School Nurse, referrals to pupil personnel specialists are made through the counselor. The team usually consists of:

Guidance Counselor
Nurse
Psychologist or Psychometrist
Social Worker
Physician
Speech Therapist
Remedial Reading Specialist
    Auxiliary Personnel
    Principal
    Assistant Principal
    Housemaster

The administrator's role in guidance. The administrator necessarily becomes involved in the pupil personnel function.

It is generally agreed that there exists a definite delineation between the disciplinary function of administration and the non-directive rapport of guidance. However, since we have suggested a revision of teacher and counselor roles, it is not incompatible for the administrator to become more personally involved with groups of students. One of the charges which have stemmed from current student unrest is the statement that administrators do not relate with students, nor do they become involved with them. It is obvious that, like the guidance counselor, the administrator must avoid the danger of remaining office-bound.

REACHING THE INDIVIDUAL THROUGH
GROUP COUNSELING

The child experiencing more serious difficulties usually finds his needs met through the aid of one or more of the specialists mentioned earlier. There is more need for services to reach that large part of the student body which is often neglected because of lack of time and personnel. In reality, the members of the pupil personnel staff are usually so extended that the preventative function is hardly implemented. The corrective or remedial function is also frequently ineffective.

One recent development which has excellent implications for the middle school is the utilization of group counseling.

Group counseling is a method by which groups of students

share common problems and voluntarily discuss and share their feelings, fears and frustrations.

The group process allows ventilation of feelings and the development of insights about oneself, sometimes through viewing others' problems. The counselor can be a reflector and facilitator of the group process.

Many problems can be effectively dealt with here, in addition to the making possible of counseling services for larger numbers of students. It is an effective way to handle normal development problems and can prevent seriously inappropriate behavior later on.

Individual and group counseling can supplement each other, with the counselor maintaining groups for certain developmental or personal problems. The school psychologist or social worker could cooperate accordingly.

How to group for interdisciplinary teaching. The interdisciplinary block, team-program is flexible by nature and can be divided into various group activities, including the following:

1. Regular class groups
2. Large or assembly groups
3. Small seminar-type group
4. Independent study

This makes possible a major departure from the procedures for grouping extant in the traditional class. In this latter situation, children are usually grouped either homogeneously or heterogeneously, usually during the summer months, and remain grouped accordingly for the entire school year. Occasionally, children experiencing difficulties may be removed from certain classes during the year and placed in remedial groups. Grouping, usually performed by the administrator, is usually based upon the grouping criteria enumerated below.

1. Standardized test scores which include achievement batteries, intelligence, and aptitude
2. Teacher recommendations and observations
3. Counselor recommendations and observations
4. Other sources of information which include student behavior, student characteristics, student environment, phy-

sical growth factors, self-development and potentialities, social adjustment, and peer relationships and status.

The dynamics of the team process and the interdisciplinary program make possible opportunities for continuous movement by students into one of the various class-organizations mentioned earlier. This, of course, involves a constant review of pupil growth by both teacher and counselor, in addition, of course, to the continued involvement of administration. Continuing diagnosis and evaluation of interests, abilities and needs, become more critical activities, shared by professional staff and students.

Meetings of the interdisciplinary team must involve consideration of student progress and assignment to appropriate activities at the proper time.

This involves a more active grouping relationship between teachers in the team, as well as with the pupil personnel staff. Dangers of the misuse of test information will require a more sophisticated understanding by teachers involved. Interpretation of grade equivalents and percentile scores on achievement tests will be helpful in determining better evaluation of the student. However, this is supplementary, since the teacher's judgments should primarily be based upon the following:

1. Class performance of student
2. Teacher-made test measures
3. Observation of behavior
4. Discussion with other team members

The counselor will then have an increased role in sharing his special competencies with the teacher-team. This can be achieved through his regular participation in team meetings and in meeting with individual teachers.

Scheduling of special programs, such as unified arts, can be administered in a manner which makes possible regular meetings of the teacher-team and of other specialists at alternate times, and with members of the pupil personnel staff.

The case conference. The case conference is particularly essential as a means of coordinating pupil personnel procedures and for personalized communications. Case studies involving teachers and pupil personnel specialists are often called to compile data, and to discuss the problems of a particular child. However, a regularly scheduled case conference should become a part of the school program. Schools may operate this on a weekly basis and involve the following: the principal; assistant principal (discipline); guidance staff; psychologist; social worker; nurse; and head teachers, as consultants.

The conference should be both preventative and remedial, and should involve follow-through procedures. Reports of the activities of supporting community agencies should be presented at this time. Two or three of the regular meetings should be devoted to periodic follow-up summaries.

The teacher should be informed, through counselors, of any specific course of action involving one of his students. The conference should be regarded as extremely confidential.

The case conference is usually employed in a centralized pupil personnel program. This is usually the optimum arrangement in the middle school.

GUIDELINES FOR USING STANDARDIZED TESTS

Data yielded from standardized tests are imperative in the type of grouping activity previously described. The following measures could be made available for a truly comprehensive student profile: (1) scholastic aptitude (I.Q.), (2) academic achievement, (3) reading — grade equivalents in speed, comprehension and vocabulary, (4) general aptitude including verbal, numerical, spatial, logical or abstract, perceptual speed (sixth graders) and mechanical aptitude (eighth graders).

Measurements should be based upon standardized tests which have been proven both *valid* and *reliable*. They should have been standardized through a large student population and must correlate with accepted and valid criteria. Teacher-made tests lack the objectivity inherent in standardized tests. A list of publishers is included in Appendix VII. Publishers will be happy to provide detailed information about their test materials, including standardization, normative procedures and statistical data.

Previous to discussing typical testing programs for a middle school, it must be emphasized that it is usually recommended that the program at any level should be sequential and part of a total program extending from elementary through high school.

This provides the benefit of the relationship of percentiles, norms and other statistical data which will aid in more graphic representation of pupil growth. This is particularly essential in the situation which encourages greater teacher participation in guidance.

THE TESTING PROGRAM, GRADES 6, 7, 8

Grades 6, 8 — intelligence testing (fall). The authors do not recommend *single factor* intelligence tests. While these are simpler to administer, they yield single I.Q. scores which are based upon a combination of verbal, numerical, spatial and logical performance areas. It is not apparent, from the single comprehensive score, in which of the areas the student has evidenced particular weaknesses or strengths Since the grouping in the interdisciplinary team situation requires phased placement into various academic areas, it is meaningless to rely on a measure which indicates a general level of scholastic aptitude.

Separate factor tests. These offer a more discriminating evaluation and can be helpful in grouping. Separate factor tests yield a total intelligence quotient but also provide separate scores. For example, the California Test of Mental Maturity (California Test Bureau) provides the following: Verbal I.Q., Numerical I.Q., and Total I.Q.

The Academic Promise Test (Psychological Corporation) offers measures in the following: Verbal; Numerical; Abstract Reasoning; Language Usage; a Nonverbal Combination score (AR + Num); a Verbal Combination score (V + LU); and a Total score.

Primary Mental Abilities Tests, or Tests of Educational Ability (SRA). These likewise yield separate scores. Consequently, a child performing on the California Test of Mental Maturity might score accordingly: Verbal I.Q., 130; Numerical I.Q., 90; Total I.Q., 110.

It is evident that the total I.Q. indicates that the student is above average in measured scholastic aptitude. The additional evidence points out his superior measurement in verbal areas, contrasted with his low-average performance in numerical areas This additional dimension is necessary in the active grouping situation.

Grades 6, 8 — achievement test (fall or spring). The achievement test is part of a sequential program. The same test series should be used in grades 6 and 8, with the primary consideration that it must relate to the overall curriculum. The interdisciplinary program, though flexible, is still bound by the general dimension, skills sequences, and measures provided in the better standardized achievement tests. Hopefully, the experiences in the program will extend beyond these in the academic preparation of each child. Nevertheless, it is important that each school carefully choose its achievement tests. Test publishers will offer assistance whenever desired. Schools may also employ the guidance or professional test-service organizations, such as Educational Records Bureau, 3 East 80th Street, New York, New York.

Grade 7 — reading survey tests. Some schools administer separate reading survey tests to the entire student body. However, these tests which measure vocabulary, rate, and comprehension, are somewhat duplicated in the 6th grade achievement battery. They are necessary for children experiencing difficulty. These are helpful in measuring student progress and are general in nature. Two examples are the Gates-MacGinitie Reading Survey Test (E) (Teachers College Press), and the Davis Reading Test, Series II (The Psychological Corporation). Diagnostic reading tests which indicate more specific reading problems are usually administered by the reading specialist.

Grade 8 — aptitude testing. The Differential Aptitude Test (Psychological Corporation) provides a comprehensive measurement of verbal, numerical, spatial, abstract reasoning, language usage, mechanical and clerical speed and accuracy, and can be helpful in academic planning for high school.

Grade 8 — interest tests. The Kuder Interest Tests, SRA, and the Mooney Problem Check-List (Psychological Corporation) can provide additional dimensions for the student's personal profile.

SUMMARY

Belief in the basic worth and dignity of the individual is the cornerstone of our way of life. Recognition of individual differences, a prime motivating factor in our educational system, is the result of the above precept. Consequently, instruction, as a basic purpose of our schools, must be supplemented by those services, skills and techniques which make it possible for the individual to function effectively and to develop his potential. The pupil personnel program can provide processes and individuals skilled in assisting each child toward achieving these goals.

nine

Evaluating the interdisciplinary program

The promise of the middle school is that the pre- and early adolescent can develop the human, conceptual, and technical capabilities which will enable him to function in an environment characterized by incredible change. This means the goals of the professional activities in the middle school center on the healthy psychological development of children so that they are open, spontaneous and secure; that they are able to communicate on a personal meaning level as well as on an informal level; that they have a sense of self-fulfillment; and that they have learned how to learn.

Interdisciplinary programs in the middle school which capture the best of team teaching and team planning, individualized instruction, and nongradedness, provide one successful approach which can achieve these goals. Yet how do we know if we have been successful or not? How do we measure a student's growth and how do we measure the effectiveness of the educational program?

Evaluation is an essential tool of human and institutional growth and development. It should be used not only to measure outcomes, but it must be used in much broader ways, such as a process of ongoing monitoring. As a monitoring process, the feedback gives a measure of the effectiveness of the processes used in reaching the final outcomes. Such an ongoing evaluation can determine the focus of instruction or the direction a particular program is taking and whether or not it needs to be altered. In all these measures, however, the assessment of growth must be carried out in relation to previously established ends.

It is imperative that evaluation not be overdone or overburdened. As a number of other factors in American education, such as teaching, curriculum, scheduling, grouping, etc., evaluation too is open to criticism. It must be reexamined in the light of new notions in the process of education. The authors want to make it clear that evaluation needs to be thought of as an open, intelligent, cooperative process to further the growth and development of the individual child, the teacher, and the program. It should not be considered a weapon or a device to discover all the wrongs of a child or of a program or of teaching. The hope is that evaluation will be used in ways to assist the educative process in fulfilling the individual rather than become a set of defensive devices to control people and institutions.

EVALUATING PROGRAMS

Purposes of evaluation. The literature on the middle school is replete with strong recommendations about the need to evaluate the middle school to determine whether it will become more effective than the traditional arrangements. Typical of such a position is a statement like this:

> The question . . . of whether a middle school is a better answer for the middle years than existing educational arrangements still needs to be answered. It is particularly important that answers be given before a complete transition is made to the middle school.[1]

---

[1]Vynce A. Hines and William M. Alexander, "Evaluating the Middle School,' *The National Elementary Principal*, XLVIII: 32-36, (February, 1969).

Consider this exhortation regarding the implications of curriculum revision:

> A comprehensive investigation of such changes is imperative before a decision is reached to proceed with implementation.[2]

Indeed, a number of comparative studies have been recommended to be carried out, such as the following: pupils in middle schools when compared to their counterparts in non-middle schools will show positive significant differences in such things as self-perception, academic achievement, favorable attitudes to school, increased creativity, etc.

This concern is unquestionably in order. It *is* essential that interdisciplinary programs and other innovative programs in the middle school become more than just bandwagon attempts to alter the status quo. Any ill-conceived change can be as negative as the situation to be changed. However, the authors want to make it clear that the period of theory-building and caution, while undoubtedly important, needs to be balanced with a period of purposeful, forward-looking activity. The time is *now*, to actualize what has been generated out of a host of theory. The evidence is clear enough from our social settings that the process and practice of education including teaching, curriculum-building, organization, grouping, management, etc., are not responding to present social and cultural conditions. It would be ill-advised to wait until pilot attempts at innovation and change have been tested out by sophisticated research personnel using sophisticated research designs before needed changes in professional behavior and practice come about.

Instead of holding back on program changes, it is important to move ahead while creating an atmosphere which will allow for monitoring, assessment, and professional self-renewal. Such program evaluation would have these purposes:

1. To determine whether the purposes identified for the middle school are being achieved. This means being cognizant of ways to improve such things as the goals and objectives of the program, the methods and practices employed, and the resources used.

---

[2]Thurston A. Atkins, "It's Time for a Change — Or Is It?" *The National Elementary Principal*, XLVIII: 46-48 (February, 1969).

2. To improve the management and operation of the school and its program.

What to evaluate. If educators are to get the most out of the opportunity of the middle school, they must be in a position to make sound decisions in relation to the alternatives available to them. They must know what the alternatives are and they must be able to assess the qualities of these alternatives. This requires information. The following components of an educational program, then, need to be evaluated: goals and objectives; the nature of the student population and the community; and the curriculum.

It must be clearly established at the outset that evaluation must be accomplished in relation to objectives and not apart from them. The practice of allowing objectives and evaluation to drift apart and to go their separate ways is one of the serious paradoxes of school operation. The guidelines given below can assist educators in overcoming this condition:

a) Commonly found vague objectives should be clarified. Objectives must consider differences in the social and cultural context of the school. Objectives and evaluation procedures are necessarily based on analysis of the nature of the community served by the school.

b) The effort to state objectives in teams of behavioral and measurable outcomes should be pursued. In doing so the classification of objectives according to two or three levels of generality may be necessary. Informal evaluation and subjective judgement cannot be precluded in relation to general objectives and to those involving values.

c) Evaluation should apply to process as well as to content objectives.

Self-concept evaluation. Since one of the major purposes of interdisciplinary programs in the middle school is the development of healthy self-concepts on the part of the children, it is important that the program be evaluated periodically to determine how effectively this is being achieved. Middle school advocates have suggested that children who are in a learning environment which focuses on their needs will show a more positive self-perception as well as higher achievement. Yet it should be understood that a high positive self-concept is not necessarily a foregone conclusion. Middle school educators need to find out how the milieu of the middle school has influenced the way children look at themselves.

In a study involving over 1,000 pupils in grades 6, 7, and 8, Pumerantz, Soares and Soares[3] set out to consider the following questions:

1. How does the child in grades 6, 7, and 8 look at himself?
2. How does he think his teacher looks at him?
3. How does he think his classmates look at him?
4. What kind of person would he like to be if he could change?

A variant of the self-perception instrument developed from previous research (Soares and Soares, 1965, 1966, 1969) was used in the study. The self-perception measured included the Self-Concept (how the individual believes himself to be at the moment); the Ideal Concept (how he would like to be or hopes to become); the Reflected Self — Classmates (how he thinks his classmates look at him); and the Reflected Self — Teachers (how he believes his teachers view him). These inventories could very easily be administered in middle schools interested in determining pupil self-perception.

It was interesting to note that the essential fact which emerged from the study discussed above was that pupils in middle schools consistently indicated significantly lower self-perception than those in any non-middle school setting. This should not be used as an argument against the middle school but simply evidence which would suggest some interesting possibilities about the conduct of the instructional program of the middle schools involved in the study. For example, these results may indicate that the middle schools were more concerned with academic achievement and this was approached in a way that tended to hinder the self-development of the concept. Such a study provides much to think about since ". . . a student's self-perception has an influence on his achievement, on his aspira-

---

[3] Philip Pumerantz, Anthony Soares, and Louise Soares, "A Comparative Study of Self-Perception of Middle School and Nonmiddle School Pupils," Bridgeport, Conn., The University of Bridgeport, 1969.

tions and goals, and on what he may actually attempt to do and attain in his life."[4]

View of the community. It is quite apparent that the community must be behind the development of an innovative program. Wilklow has written, "Middle school programs must be supported financially and morally by boards of education . . . if they are to be successful in meeting needs of children. There should be a full commitment by all concerned to the development, execution and continuous evaluation of the program."[5]

A successful device in developing an interrelated program would be to have an open meeting for the community where school officials will have an opportunity to inform interested and concerned groups about the new educational program. But the spin-off of such an activity should not be lost. A questionnaire should be drawn up and distributed to the participants so that they can complete it before they leave. Such a questionnaire might include such items as the following:

1. Has this meeting provided you with a better idea of how the program/school will be implemented?
2. Does the middle school program as you have heard it described here provide a suitable program for your child?
3. Would you be interested in attending future discussion groups or meetings with middle school staff members to talk about various aspects of your child and his school program?

Evaluating objectives. It is essential that the goals and objectives of the middle school program be examined as well as the other aspects of the program. Frequently it is an area which is overlooked in the evaluation process. Objectives need to be evaluated "for feasibility; consistency with what is presently known about how pupils learn; for consistency with each other; for including areas judged to be important functions of schools; for appropriateness for the pupil population and community

---

[4] *Ibid.*

[5] Leighton B. Wilklow, "Five Principles for Establishing and Operating a Middle School," *Dissemination Services on the Middle Grades,* Educational Leadership Institute, Inc., Vol. II, No. 3, October, 1970.

served; for being trivial; and for consistency with the democratic tradition."[6]

When considering an assessment of objectives, the criteria should be how appropriate they are for pre- and early adolescents. The following are examples of appropriate objectives that are suggested for middle schools·

1. We should attempt to lessen competition. The middle school should not be a carbon copy of the high school.
2. We should stress individual achievement at the student's own level.
3. We should emphasize personal guidance services.
4. We should aid the development of the self-image, and thus prepare pupils for the greater competitiveness in the senior high school.
5. We should provide greater exploratory opportunities.
6. We should organize a school that is child-centered rather than subject-centered
7. We should provide opportunities to learn self-direction.
8. We should provide greater chances for pupils to interact with their peers.
9. We should select student-oriented rather than subject-oriented teachers.

Evaluating curriculum. In order to evaluate the success of an educational program, progress of the program must be measured in relation to definitive educational objectives. The development of objectives provides the guidance for determining the strategies, tactics and techniques for fulfilling the educational program for middle school youngsters. Curricular decisions should be made on the basis of specific program objectives which then need to undergo an ongoing monitoring process. The following objectives are illustrative of the kind that can be a "lighthouse" for curriculum development:

1. To understand the relationship between environment and knowledge

---

[6]V.A. Hines, "Perspectives on Evaluation," Middle School Portfolio, Leaflet No. XIII, Association for Childhood Educational International, Washington, D.C., 1968.

2. To understand that learning is not preparation for life but life itself
3. To understand the interrelationship of discipline
4. To understand the tentativeness of knowledge
5. To understand one's self
6. To understand the dimensions of freedom and restraint
7. To be enthusiastic for learning
8. To appreicate esthetics, sensitivity, and judgement
9. To respect the values of others
10. To appreciate the interaction of authority and individual and group responsibilities
11. To appreciate the use of leisure time.

In order to determine how effective the middle school curriculum is, one might develop an instrument which can provide such information. Is the curriculum consistent with the objectives established and with the nature of the pupils being served?

A fine illustration of an evaluation instrument for a middle school program is to be found in the proceedings of a middle school workshop held in Carmel, N.Y.[7] In the instrument which follows, the respondent has the opportunity of rating on a continuum from high to low or excellent to poor or whichever applies:

PROGRAM

1. To what extent did this program provide opportunity for individualized instruction?
2. To what extent was there opportunity provided for independent study?
3. To what extent did this program enable children to meet success in relation to their own abilities academically?
4. To what degree did this program enable children to meet success in relation to their own social development?
5. To what extent did this program enable you to know and understand your students better?
6. Is there any evidence that the transition to grade seven was more effective than in previous programs?

---

[7]Report of Middle School Workshop, Carmel Central School District No. 2, Carmel, N.Y., July, 1969, pp. 15-25.

7. To what extent did you find this program provided efficient use of time?

8. To what extent did this program affect your coverage of prescribed curriculum?

9. To what extent was there correlation between subject lines?

10. Strong correlation between subject lines occurred where?

11. What effect did the program have on student discipline?

12. How did the program provide for the locating and accounting of students?

13. What effect did the program have on student responsibility?

14. What effect did the program have on student respect for authority?

15. What effect did the program have on student leadership?

16. What effect did the program have on student attitudes towards academic subjects?

17. What effect did the program have on student attitudes toward extra-curricular and co-curricular activities?

18. What effect did the program have on student attitudes towards self?

19. What effect did the program have on student attitudes toward peers?

20. What effect did the program have on student anxiety?

21. How well were the students able to utilize independent study time?

22. How effective was the program with innovations and changes?

23. Did the program allow for teacher control of innovations?

24. Did the program allow for team control of innovations?

25. What was the effect of the program on morale among the team teachers?

26. In the cooperative teaching situation, did the program lend itself to the accommodation of differences in the program and techniques of colleagues?

27. In the cooperative situation, did the program lend itself to the accommodation of differences in personalities of colleagues?

28. In the cooperative teaching situation, did the program lend itself to the differences in philosophies of colleagues?

29. In the cooperative teaching situation, did the program lend itself to the accommodation of differences in dis cipline criteria of colleagues?

30. Have your instructional patterns changed because of this program?

31. Did the program permit more time for planning?

32. Did the program lend itself to an effective use of audio-visual equipment?

33. Did the program lend itself to a greater opportunity for interdisciplinary instruction?

34. Would you recommend continuing this program on the basis of your experience?

EVALUATING TEACHING

Self-appraisal. If the purpose of the interdisciplinary program in the middle school is to fulfill the individual child, then it is important that teachers be prepared to examine how effective they are with children. Evaluating teaching in the soundest sense means a self-evaluation, a self-appraisal. In turn, this can help instruction focus on the needs of pupils. To be the most effective, teachers need to be aware of their strengths and weaknesses so that they can truly respond to pupils.

An excellent rating device which teachers in the middle schools can use in order to determine how effectively they are meeting needs of pupils is suggested in the model of the Pennsylvania School Study Council:[8]

EVALUATION OF NEEDS

Needs of Middle School Students	Present Assessment	Explanation
1. To experience affection, security, and humor from adults.		

[8]John W. Kohl, William E. Caldwell, and Donald H. Eichhorn, "Self-Appraisal and Development of the Middle School: An Inservice Approach," The Pennsylvania School Study Council, Inc., July, 1970, pp. 17-20.

EVALUATION OF NEEDS

Needs of Middle School Students	Present Assessment	Explanation
2. To gain insight into their own aptitudes		
3. To acquire empathy for the attitudes of others and to be recognized and have their efforts acknowledged.		
4. To understand and maintain mental and physical health.		
5. To experience success frequently.		
6. To attain basic skills and understandings.		
7. To develop an appreciation of the ideals of democracy.		
8. To develop wholesome leisure time activities.		
9. To understand wholesome home and family relationships.		
10. To develop effective learning skills.		
11. To receive assistance in personal and social adjustment.		
12. To understand and use the problem solving approach.		
13. To gain insight with respect to other races, creeds and cultures.		
14. To develop a sense of values with respect to material things.		
15. To develop understanding of desirable human relationships.		
16. To develop an awareness of society beyond the community.		
17. To have aesthetic experiences which enrich appreciations.		

EVALUATION OF NEEDS

Needs of Middle School Students	Present Assessment	Explanation
18. To understand the need for self-reliance.		
19. To develop a sense of self-discipline.		
20. To learn to differentiate between the real and the vicarious.		
21. To learn to set goals and to develop the incentive necessary to reach them.		
22. To develop personal acceptance and understanding of the irregularities of the physical and emotional changes of transience.		
23. To acquire a greater sense of responsibility for personal possessions.		
24. To encourage respect for virtues of honesty and sincerity.		
25. To participate in school activities and groups.		

For a specific indication of how effective middle school teachers are with pupils, consider this self-appraisal below dealing with an independent study program. Here the teacher has the opportunity of eliciting information about some of the dimensions of this type of instructional arrangement:

1. How many students signed up for independent study in your area?
2. How many students that started a program completed their project?
3. Did you find the independent work of higher quality than the conventional work?
4. What original groups did these students come from?

5. Complete the attached table, listing the information for each project undertaken.
   a. Indicate the title or topic of the study.
   b. What were the criteria for success for this study?
   c. Where, physically, was this study carried on?
   d. List approximate percentage of time spent in each area.
   e. If possible, list the materials the student needed but did not have access to.
6. How many students sought special help during the six-week period! What kind of special help did they need?

EVALUATING STUDENTS

Focusing on the individual. The development of interdisciplinary programs in the middle schools ultimately is geared to the self-fulfillment of the individual child. The total process of the school — instruction, curriculum, organization, guidance, management, etc. — should be centered around the achievement of this position. Therefore, evaluation, too, must be set up so that this idea can reach fruition.

The achievement of a positive self-concept on the part of middle school pupils must be a primary goal of the educational program. A poor concept suggests lack of confidence in facing oneself and mastering the environment. And these in turn affect the quality of the school performance. Since the formative years of self-concept development occur during the time of pre- and early adolescence, it is reasonable to assume that teachers and other elements in the middle school environment play a significant role in the development of the view students have of themselves. A number of traditional approaches to teaching such as rigid grouping and continuous lecturing have tended to serve as constraints to the development of the self-concept and prevent positive learning from occurring.

There is a growing body of evidence which shows that the genuine feeling that a person has about himself and his situation is a good predictor of academic success. Individualized instruction, independent study, personal development, learning skills, and other such areas, are based on the importance of the self-concept and a person's achievement and general success. The question then becomes: Can an individual's view of himself be enhanced by giving him the kind of environment and program in which he can succeed? If this can occur, one may probably perform at a higher level. A person who has a low opinion of himself may find it difficult to do well.[9]

In this light, then, it is important to realize that evaluations of the pupil by the teacher must be handled carefully and judiciously. Frequently, teacher-made tests reflect the idea of teacher-determined curriculum and choices. The interdisciplinary program in the middle school suggests that teacher and pupil share in the determination of the curriculum and learning outcomes. This means, therefore, that the student should also become involved with the process of self-evaluation. For example, the view a student feels a teacher has of him may cause him to lose sight of his own objectives and role and indeed may cause him to develop an unhealthy individual concept. Lee has suggested that

> . . if there can be significant communication between the evaluator and the evaluated, common goals can be identified and common purposes accepted and progress toward these recognized by both. To the extent that this occurs, the evaluation can become useful and can contribute to further development in line with the individual's goals. As the evaluator respects the individuality and purposes of the learner, the evaluator's reactions can be contributive rather than harmful . . . . Indeed evaluative interaction can be a positive force in personal development.[10]

Gathering data on students. Educational leaders need to gather information about middle school pupils in order to determine how effective are the goals and objectives of the overall school program as we saw earlier. In addition, individual teachers need to gather information about their students, to give them information about the success of their instruction.

---

[9]Philip Pumerantz, Anthony Soares, and Louise Soares, "A Comparative Study of the Self-Perceptions of Middle School and Nonmiddle School Pupils," Bridgeport, Conn.: University of Bridgeport, 1969.

[10]Dorris May Lee, "Teaching and Evaluation," in *Evaluation as Feedback and Guide*, ed. by Fred T. Wilhelms. Washington, D.C.: Association for Supervision and Curriculum Development, 1967, p. 84.

Keep in mind that the gathering of information should be put into the context of in-put for instructional improvement rather than for intimidation of the students.

To get the information from students, for example, about how they feel they might benefit from an interdisciplinary program, one might consider an instrument such as the following: In this survey the teacher has an opportunity to make comments on twenty characteristics ranging all the way from the quality of the child's work to the child's perception of his academic potential.

A. The child's work is typically
1. prompt
2. late
3. incomplete
4. thorough
5. careless
6. neat
7. sloppy
8. imaginative
9. perfunctory

B. The child has difficulty doing assignments which are
1. short, clear, and routine
2. long-range, with ample teacher direction
3. long-range, with direction left to pupil
4. to be done in writing
5. to be reported orally
6. anything out of the ordinary
7. (rarely does homework of any kind)

C. During in-school working periods, the child typically
1. applies himself consistently and efficiently
2. applies himself consistently but not efficiently
3. works well for short periods only
4. needs to be "made" to stay at the job
5. habitually disturbs his peers

D. Work, for this child, seems to be
1. an unpleasant necessity to be avoided or dispensed with quickly
2. usually dull, only occasionally of interest
3. a way to win his teacher's approval
4. a way to win his parents' approval

  5. a way to win his peers' approval
  6. important as a means of self-improvement
  7. important as a means toward a long-range goal

E. In trying to solve a learning problem, the child has difficulty

  1. perceiving the problem
  2. developing problem-solving strategies
  3. organizing data
  4. making generalizations
  5. testing generalizations
  6. remembering facts
  7. remembering ideas
  8. working with concrete materials
  9. working with abstractions

F. When faced with an "open-minded" situation where there are no "right" answers, the child

  1. tends to panic and withdraw
  2. becomes irritable and demands "the answers"
  3. remains calm but is unable to hypothesize
  4. makes wild guesses without knowing how to test them
  5. formulates hypotheses and devises means for testing them

G. In a well-defined situation where answers are either right or wrong, the child's thinking is ordinarily

  1. logical
  2. illogical
  3. accurate
  4. erratic
  5. hampered by anxiety
  6. uneven—occasionally accurate and occasionally irrelevant

H. The child reveals the extent of his curiosity by

  1. doing only the work assigned
  2. asking thoughtful questions
  3. pursuing other source materials or experiences
  4. relating the work at hand to other experiences
  5. following through consistently on matters of individual interest

I. In class, the child relates to his peers with

1. enthusiasm
2. cooperation
3. leadership
4. confidence
5. anxiety—apprehension
6. belligerence
7. laziness
8. withdrawal

J. When not in class, the child

1. exhibits considerable vitality
2. withdraws from association with others
3. assumes leadership role
4. is gregarious and cooperative
5. becomes aggressive
6. does not consider the needs of others
7. engages in personal interests and activities
8. doesn't know what to do

K. When free, the child is most often found

1. with one or two close friends
2. with the same group of friends
3. with a variety of acquaintances
4. with adults rather than peers
5. alone

L. The child's peers regard him with

1. respect
2. liking a desire for association
3. ridicule
4. suspicion
5. toleration
6. admiration
7. indifference

M. In school, the child's attitude towards his parents is one of

1. pride and affection
2. hostility
3. submissiveness—seems strongly directed by parents
4. embarrassment
5. alternate pride and rebellion

N. In his relationships with teachers, the child

1. constantly seeks the teacher's companionship and reassurance
2. avoids being alone with a teacher
3. consults teachers only in exceptional situations
4. relates naturally and easily to teachers
5. seeks the attention of special personnel (counselor, librarian, etc.)

O. In his attitudes toward the adult world, the child

1. is strongly motivated by adult approval
2. exhibits a marked antipathy toward adults
3. seeks a behavior pattern that is markedly independent of adult influence
4. is strongly motivated by his peers
5. has a nice balance in his desires for adult and peer approval

P. In general, the child seems to relate best with adults who are

1. male
2. female
3. older
4. younger
5. calm
6. energetic
7. well-organized
8. creative
9. authoritarian
10. libertarian

Q. The child regards himself physically as

1. attractive
2. unattractive
3. well-developed
4. underdeveloped
5. strong, energetic
6. weak
7. apprehensive about future growth and development
8. confident about future growth and development

R. The child believes that his peers see him as

1. well-liked, a potential friend
2. disliked, one to be avoided whenever possible

   3. someone not usually noticed

   4. opinionated

   5. gregarious

   6. quarrelsome

   7. intelligent

   8. attractive

   9. reliable

 10. artistic

S. The child feels that teachers and other adults see him as

   1. polite and well-mannered

   2. withdrawn

   3. silly

   4. humorous

   5. bright

   6. dull

   7. contrary

   8. boisterous

   9. nervous

 10. confident

T. The child perceives his academic potential as

   1. superior

   2. adequate

   3. limited to certain areas

   4. restricted because of certain skill deficiencies[11]

It is also important, obviously, to gather information about the academic achievement of the pupils. In order to get additional important information about the middle school program, one must discover the extent to which children in the middle schools score higher on the standardized achievement tests than children in the same grades in controlled situations. One might hypothesize that middle school students will achieve significantly higher results on standardized tests than nonmiddle school pupils.

Of course, there are additional creative ways of gathering data about middle school pupils. The only constraint to this lies within the vision of the middle school teachers themselves.

---

[11] "Fox Lane Middle School Pupil Characteristic Survey," Fox Lane Middle School, Bedford, N.Y.

SUMMARY

Evaluation was viewed from the point of view of gathering data about humans and institutions. It can be a helpful tool in giving information about the strengths and weaknesses of the educational program and about the processes carried on by teachers. Yet, the essential point which was stressed is that evaluation should not be overburdened and carried out in ways that would defeat the educative progress. Since the ends of the interdisciplinary middle school is to achieve the fulfillment of the individual, evaluation then must be examined in this light. Evaluation must be used to facilitate learning rather than become a controlled device to hinder it.

Lesson plan for a grade six unit
on "discovering who I am"[1]

DISCOVERING WHO I AM is a six-week interdisciplinary unit for sixth grade students which will integrate literature, social studies, art, music, semantics, and media. The unit is made up of six sections. "I've Got A Name," "Brothers, Sisters, Mothers, Fathers, and All Those Relatives," "The Other Kids," "Sticks and Stones," "Mirrors and Doors—The Arts," and "The Inner Space Program." Each section consists of selected readings with analytical questions. The purpose of the readings and the questions is to lead students to experiences which will help them define the meaning of the word "humanities," arouse in them interests in the arts and the media, help them see themselves as human beings in a world of human beings.

All of the material in this unit is designed to be taught inductively. That is, the student is presented with a wealth of data which he uses to come to some conclusion, explanation, or interpretation of the material at hand. The student is then expected to develop his

---

[1]Jack Strauss, Richard Doufour, and Stephen Smith, "Discovering Who I Am: A Humanities Course for Sixth Grade Students," *Elementary English*, January, 1970, pp. 85-120. Copyright © by the Nat'l Council of Teachers of English. Reprinted by permission of authors and publisher.

own interpretation through skillful use of inquiry methods. The teacher's task is to guide the student to his answers. Thus, lesson plans provide suggestions as to how this task may be carried out. The following is the plan for section one, "I've Got a Name":

I'VE GOT A NAME

Knowledge Objective:	to know that the humanities help us understand and devise the many roles we play as we develop an identity.
Affective Objective:	to appreciate that everyone is both an "I" and a "He"; to recognize the uniqueness and variety of each human personality.
Inquiry Objective:	to be able to separate feelings from knowledge; to be able to recognize how one's own frame of reference influences and shapes thinking, feelings and actions.
Materials:	Charlie Brown Kit "I've Got a Name" by Zachary Gold (Basic Text—I'VE GOT A NAME) Series of Opening pictures in the Basic Text WHO DO YOU THINK YOU ARE, CHARLIE BROWN? "Blind Men and the Elephant" (Student handout) "The Influence Chart" (Student handout) Shock—Record of mood music

Suggested Strategies

Distribute WHO DO YOU THINK YOU ARE, CHARLIE BROWN? (To be used in class only)

Distribute the "Charlie Brown Kit." Includes: 1. Charlie Brown Bone Structure, 2. The Charlie Brown Notebook.

Have students look only at front and back covers to get the "feel" of the book. Note that the covers deal with the problem of identity for Charlie Brown and point out that this is the main concern of the unit which the class is beginning.

Note: The teacher should plan to use a cartoon a day from this book. The order is not important but it might be easier to follow the sequence in the book. A flexible ritual should be established with the same time each day and the same four basic steps which are as follows:

1. Student should read the complete strip.
2. Complete the Charlie Brown Bone Structure using the evidence of this cartoon only.
3. State in a sentence in the "Charlie Brown Notebook" something about Charlie's attitude toward people or people's attitude toward Charlie.
4. In a paragraph state your feelings about the incident in the cartoon.

Pass out I'VE GOT A NAME.

Allow students time to glance through the book. Student questions and comments should lead to a discussion of the Humanities and the kind of work they will be doing for the six-week unit. The teacher should indicate that the readings will be guided through class discussions and the use of a record which supplements the text.

Have the class turn to the pictures at the beginning of the text.

Ask, "What do all the pictures have in common?" "What moods do you find on the faces?" "What stories do some of the pictures remind you of?" Teachers should allow free play in the answers. No predetermined response should be looked for. Suggest that the class will be looking at faces throughout the six-week unit. As students react to the "stories" behind the faces, the teacher should suggest that what a face suggests is in part what we see and in part what we are willing to see. This suggestion will lead into the next activity.

Have student enter class with a note as pre-arranged. When he has left, ask the class to describe the incident that has just occurred. What happened? Who did it? What did he wear? Look like? Weight? Height?

Pre-arrange for a student or teacher to come into the room, smile as he hands you a note, frown and mutter as you write a reply which he reads, lifts his right foot and limps out of the room. Give students about five minutes to write on scratch paper what happened. Send student to board to record what happened, mannerisms of the person— height, weight, etc. Show class how varied answers are and raise the question as to some of the reasons which account for the differences. Does what we see depend on who we are and where we are?

Pass out "The Blind Men and the Elephant"

Arrange to read the poem by having one student read the narrative sections, and assigning the quoted dialogue to six other students.

When the reading has been concluded, ask for reactions to the final two lines of the poem.

When someone has indicated that if each man's version were added to all the others', a correct picture would emerge. Have students get out paper and try to draw the elephant from the six descriptions. Discussion should suggest dangers inherent in making judgments on limited experience.

Summarize some of the reactions in the previous two exercises which suggest how personal background and experience affected judgments.

"Where do your ideas come from?"

Teacher goes to blackboard and jots down student answers to this question.

"Which of the items on the list is most influential"?

Home, church, friends, school, books, radio, T-V, magazines.

Hand out Influence Chart

Teacher should stimulate divergent thinking but the unstructured form should result in no consensus. After the discussion has gone on for a few minutes, the teacher should hand out the "Influence Chart." After instructions, 10 or 15 minutes should be allowed to fill out the chart. Using a prepared transparency, fill out a master sheet with a grease pencil of the responses. As results are recorded, teacher should be working toward the point that there is no agreement as to where the "real" influences are. Why?

Play one side of the record *Shock*. Students are to indicate answers to "Where is it happening"? Who is involved"? and "What is happening"?

As students discuss responses, the teacher should direct attention to the variety of responses and raise the question of how background and experiences may account for the differences.

Three-Dimensional Portrait
(Charlie Brown)

I. Appearance

    a. Sex_____

    b. Age _____

    c. Height and weight_____

    d. Color of hair, eyes, skin _____

    e. Posture_____

    f. General (good looking—skinny—heavy—clean, neat, untidy, shape of head, face, limbs, birthmarks, freckles, defects)

    _____

    _____

    _____

II. Background

    a. Poor, rich, average standard of living_____

    b. Position or occupation _____

    c. Education: amount, kinds of schools, marks, favorite subjects, poorest subjects, aptitudes _____

    _____

    _____

    _____

d. Home life _____

_____

_____

_____

e. Religion_____
f. Race—nationality _____
g. Place in community: leader among friends, clubs, sports_____

_____

_____

h. Political affiliations_____

_____

i. Amusements, hobbies: books, newspapers, magazines_____

_____

_____

_____

_____

III. Ideas
1. Standards of right and wrong_____

_____

_____

2. Personal premise, ambition_____

_____

_____

3. Frustrations, chief disappointments_____

_____

_____

4. Temperament: easy going, pessimistic, optimistic_____

_____

_____

5. Attitude toward life: resigned, militant, defeatist_____

_____

_____

6. Abilities_____

_____

_____

7. Qualities: imagination, judgment, taste, poise__

_____

_____

_____

_____

_____

_____

appendix ii

Working paper educational specifications--middle school[1]

CURRICULUM AREA————————————

A. PHILOSOPHY OF AREA

B. FUNCTION OF AREA

---

[1]Educational Specification Working Paper — Branford Board of Education, Branford, Connecticut. (Undated; Mimeographed.)

C. SPACE FACILITIES REQUIRED   Approximate   Approximate
   1. Number and Type of Room.   Dimensions   Total Area
     a.
     b.
     c.

D. DESCRIPTION OF FACILITIES
   1. Location.
     a.
     b.
     c.
   2. Walls.
     a. Flag holder
     b. Painted, soft pastel
     c. Molding around wall for hanging displays
     d. If possible, one wall to be sound-proof and movable
     e. Approximately _____ lineal feet of vertical movable chalkless chalkboard located on the front wall with approximately _____ lineal feet of tack board and _____ lineal feet of chalkboard permanently installed on the wall behind the vertical chalkboard
     f. One 60" x 60" screen mounted on the front wall with extension brackets for overhead as well as other projection
     g. Tackboard
     h.
     i.
     j.
     k.
   3. Floors.
     a. Carpeting
     b.
     c.
   4. Ceiling.
     a. Acoustical tile
     b.
     c.
   5. Windows and Blinds.
     a. High windows to provide more usable exterior wall space
     b. (Draperies)   (Blinds with slat runners)_____ installed in such a manner so that the room can be darkened as much as possible
     c.
     d.

6. Built-in Equipment and Storage Areas.
   a. Teacher wardrobe (including file) with lock.
   b. Cabinet space
   c. Open shelving:
   d.
   e.
   f.
   g.
7. Other Equipment
   a.
   b.
   c.
   d.
   e.
   f.
   g.
   h.
8. Mechanical and Utility Needs
   a. Lighting
      i. Fluorescent, 70 candle power
      ii.
      iii.
   b. Electrical and Other Utility Services
      i. Sufficient duplex outlets (3 prong, grounded) along each wall to permit a wide and varied use of different audio-visual machines
      ii. Two built-in sound speakers, acoustically arranged
      iii. Telephone jacks for home-bound instruction
      iv. Closed circuit television cable
      v. Telephone intercom with main office
      vi. Public address speaker connection with main office
      vii. Clock and program chime synchronized with master clock and program unit
      viii.
      ix.
      x.
   c. Heating and ventilating
      i. Air-conditioning
      ii. Thermostat with individual controls
      iii. A system built-in and arranged in a manner to utilize the minimum amount of necessary wall space
      iv.
      v.

8. Mechanical and Utility Needs. (continued)
   d. Plumbing
      i
      ii.
      iii

A model chronology for moving to a middle school[1]

PHASE 1 – Summer

   A. *Workshop on Day One*

      Areas of presentation by consultants:
      1. Characteristics of youngsters of middle school age
      2. Rationale for the middle school program
      3. Description of practices used in middle schools
      4. Models of middle school programs
      5. A suggested chronology for the development of the middle school program in Mifflin County

   B. *Workshop on Day Two*

      1. Review basic middle school rationale
      2. Initiate plans to establish a steering committee for the development of the middle school program
      3. Establish a chronology for the next two-year period

---

[1]Formulated by a committee of teachers and principals at workshop meetings on June 19 and July 29 of 1970, Mifflin County School District, Pennsylvania.

PHASE 2 — First Inservice Day of Fall

A. Provide general orientation of the nature of the middle school program to all members of the professional staff.

B. After consultant presents an overview of the nature of the middle school program, the faculty will be broken down into subgroups with steering committee members serving as group leaders. The purpose of the subgroup meetings is to discuss areas presented by the consultant and prepare questions in writing for the consultant to answer at the reconvened general meeting.

PHASE 3 — Second Inservice Day

A. The summer workshop participants who indicated a willingness to serve on the steering committee will be involved in this phase of development. Other teachers interested in the middle school program will also be members of the steering committee.

B. Develop a steering committee and subcommittees.

C. Set up committees to investigate and present curriculum and establish basic beliefs in each subject area.

D. Set up committees to explore instructional techniques—scheduling, grouping, team teaching, and other areas of middle school programs.

E. Plan to have some committee members, especially those who will become directly involved in the middle school program, visit middle schools between October 12 and November 11. Develop pre-plans for school visitations, i.e., plans that spell out what we are looking for.

PHASE 4 — Third Inservice Day

A. Plan to develop a current status notebook (report of developments thus far) for each committee member.

B. Survey building needs and recommend spacing modifications.

C. Survey the administrative and teaching staff needed in each building.

D. Committees will report on scheduling, grouping, team teaching, evaluation procedures, school visitations, and other pertinent areas.

E. Select consultants and set up an agenda for them to follow at the Spring meeting.

PHASE 5 — Fourth Inservice Day

A. At this meeting the teachers and principal of a middle school in operation will be brought in as consultants to discuss scheduling, grouping, staffing, evaluation, and other procedures.
B. Update the current status notebook.
C. Recommend groups to be formed for the next summer Inservice Program.
D. Decide, in the light of planning achievements thus far, as to whether the appropriate starting time for informing parents of the middle school program should take place during the next summer or the fall.

PHASE 6 — Second Summer

A. To help in developing the total curriculum program, bring boys and girls in for a discussion with the committee (students going into the 6th and 9th grades, as well as 7th and 8th graders).
B. Director of Middle Schools and subcommittee will spend a full five-day period in developing a proposed curriculum.

PHASE 7 — Inservice Days of the year

A. Use sociogram techniques to determine composition of teams within each school.
B. Complete selection of staff members for each school.
C. Complete curriculum guides and the development of the total program in preparation for the opening of school in September.
D. Complete scheduling, grouping, evaluation, and other necessary procedures for the opening of school in the following September.
E. Involve parents in orientation to the middle school program — not all parents at once, but in smaller groups such as grade levels in geographic areas.
F. Involve incoming 6th, 7th, and 8th grade students in orientation to the middle school program.

PHASE 8 — Third Summer

A. One-week workshop for total staff:
   1. *Run through a simulated schedule of a day's program.* (Some students could be involved in this program.)
   2. Total staff observation and evaluation of simulated activities.
B. Develop plans for a more detailed orientation program for the following September for the students and staff of each building.

Proposal for a one-week
middle school workshop[1]

PROGRAM

Workshop Goals: To have a chance to continue to upgrade the current practice of instruction and leadership on the junior high-middle school level through the implementation of an authentic middle school program.

Day One

Morning:

A. Overview of the workshop (lecture-discussion—informal)
Loosening-up session
Planning of study groups (mixed-role teams)

B. General overview of the authentic middle school
What are the (new) possibilities for teaching, guidance, administration?
Securing the philosophy; dealing with the assumptions (reverse brainstorming)

---

[1] Proposal for a One-week Middle School Workshop, Norwalk, Connecticut Public School, Summer, 1970. (Mimeographed.)

Afternoon:

Meeting of teams with catalysts (group work)
On developing a philosophy (the Assumptions again)
Begin to design some pilot situations for September for each building

Day Two

Morning:

A. Designing and implementing an "Individualized Self-fulfillment Program" for students in ages 11-13. (Small group sessions + large group coalition put together.)
1. Firming up what we know about these children
2. Some tentative agreements on what they need to learn, i.e., cognitive, affective, skills (involve students in this).
3. What are the instructional and administrative procedures to carry this out?

Afternoon:

Designing the procedures
Organizing for teaching
Team teaching
Individualized instruction
Presentation — lecture
Group designing sessions

Day Three

Morning:

Developing interdisciplinary team teaching
Team role
Administrator's role
Teacher's role
Guidance counselor's role
Curriculum coordinator's role
Develop a model interdisciplinary theme, e.g., *Aggression*

Afternoon:

Individualized instruction
Organizing and initiating independent study
Student selection and project evaluation
Interdisciplinary approach to individual instruction
Examples of successful approaches

Day Four

Morning:

Flexible scheduling (a fulfilling vehicle, a means not an end)
Presentation lecture
Personalize what was learned or design-workshop
Modular schedules to achieve individual self-fulfillment
Consultant and local talent

Afternoon:

Scheduling and grouping practices
Use of time
Use of facilities
Criteria for grouping

Day Five

Morning:

The role of the building principal
Responsibilities delegated to staff
Decisions regarding team leaders and operation of the team
Hiring and recruiting practices
Inservice professional development responsibilities

Afternoon:

Summary and review of workshop
Plan follow-up activities
Pilot projects in September
Evaluation of workshop by participants

WORKSHOP PROCEDURE

The workshop characteristically should be informal, open and flexible. Each day might start at 9:00 a.m. and close at 3:00 p.m. The program topics should suggest parameters within which the participants can begin to assume the responsibility of deciding the most germane areas of study for them. Basically, the theme could be individual self-fulfillment. Participants and consultants can decide on and design the procedures necessary to realize this broad aim.

Brief presentations can be made by consultants to the large group and then small groups could have the chance, in the late morning and afternoon to personalize what they have heard. Consultants can be available throughout the day. Practical working sessions using worksheets and other materials should be a standard mode of instruction.

The outcome of these sessions should be some concrete steps to change some significant processes in teaching and administration. Hopefully, it should be possible to get each person to be committed to piloting a new approach appendix v

Independent study--grade six--
east house

Dear Sixth Grade East House Students:

We would like to give each one of you the chance to study on your own any topic or subject in which you might be interested for a period of one to two weeks. This Independent Study Project, as we are calling it, would possibly free you from attending all of your classes, except physical education, for the length of time mentioned above.

We are offering you this possibility for a new kind of learning experience because we feel that all of you at one time or another this year have exhibited enough maturity, enthusiasm, and willingness to learn to be able now to make some of your own decisions regarding what and how you personally might wish to study. All of you must have some particular subject, topic, hobby, or interest that, if given the chance, you would like to find out a great deal more about. And now you may have the chance.

To begin, there are just two things that you must do: 1. think seriously about this letter and the opportunities it might hold for you; and 2. fill out in as much detail as possible the attached "Proposal for Independent Study," sign it, and return it to your home room teacher by the date prescribed. Then the following "Independent Study Time-Table" will have gone — and will continue to go — into effect:

14 April, Monday   — independent study concept presented to students

18 April, Friday   — proposals due to home room teachers

Week of 18 April to 24 April — proposals considered by team and special representatives; advisors assigned

25 April, Friday   — students notified of acceptance and assigned advisor; accepted students contact all their teachers with a "Letter of Re-introduction"

28 April, Monday   — for one week minimum to two weeks minimum, Independent Study Project I begins

Three things must be said at this point. First, your proposal is wide open: you may wish to propose to learn about a certain topic using the facilities of the library; you might want to make or do something which would be a particular challenge using the more specialized equipment in unified arts, science classrooms (when available), or the music or foreign language or communications departments; you might simply propose to do something at the middle school which you feel is important to you now, for which you would not otherwise have the time, given your busy academic schedule; or you might feel that you are particularly weak in one or more areas of your academic program and would like special help and special materials set up just for you for a 1-2 week period. All of these are possibilities; it is up to you to decide on the basis of your interests and self-knowledge just what you would like to propose to do.

Secondly, if your proposal is accepted (and more will be said about this in the next paragraph), your relationship with your advisor will be most important in the period of time that you are working on your own. It will be up to you two to decide such things as: what will be the end-product (if any) of your independent study? — in other words, what will you have to show at the end of one or two weeks? how will your work be evaluated? — or will it? how often and when will meetings with your advisor be arranged; where will your study headquarters be located? — or — how can you be contacted if necessary? Others of your teachers can also get in touch with your advisor if the need arises — and he or she will in turn get in touch with you. For these reasons, the choice of assignment of an advisor should be very important to you.

Thirdly, and finally, a word about the proposal selection process: how might you be chosen to work independently? The people involved in reading and making the final selection of all proposals submitted will be representatives from the various departments. The final selection process will be based on the proposals which you submit; they will be read and evaluated, using such criteria as forethought, depth and specificity, organization, originality, enthusiasm, and sincerity — in no particular order. Your past grades and various abilities will in no way hinder your chances for selection. In other words, don't expect that only "smart kids" will be chosen to work independently, for that very simply will not be the case.

One final word . . . . We should tell you in advance that not everyone who submits a proposal will automatically have the chance to study independently. To begin, we feel we must limit the number of students involved at any one time — simply because there are other students from other houses doing the same thing, and the middle school just does not yet have the facilities or the personnel to allow every student to study this way. If all works out well, however, during Independent Study Project I, there is no reason why Projects II, III, and IV, etc., cannot follow before the school year is over.[1]

---

[1] Provided by Dr. Malcolm Rizzutto, Fox Lane Middle School, Bedford, N.Y. (Mimeographed; April, 1969.)

List of simulations appropriate for middle school pupils

Adventuring — Abt Associates, Inc.
Bushman Exploring and Gathering — Educational Development Center.
Campaign — Instructional Simulations, Inc.
Caribou Hunting — Educational Development Center.
Compass-Community Priority Assessment Simulation — Instructional Simulations, Inc.
Democracy (Legislature) — Western Publishing Company, Inc.
Disaster — Western Publishing Company, Inc.
Economic System — Western Publishing Company, Inc.
Economy — Abt Associates, Inc.
The English Civil War Unit — Abt Associates, Inc.
Generation Gap — Western Publishing Company, Inc.
Ghetto — Western Publishing Company, Inc.
Impact — A Community Simulation — Instructional Simulations Inc.
Life Career — Western Publishing Company, Inc.
Neighborhood — Abt Associates, Inc.
Panic — Interact.
Pollution — Abt Associates, Inc.
Sierra Leone — Abt Associates, Inc.
The Slave Trade Game — Abt Associates, Inc.

appendix vii

Sources for educational and psychological tests typically used in the middle school

California Test Bureau
5916 Hollywood Boulevard
Los Angeles, California 90028

Publishers of California Test of Mental Maturity, California Reading Test, and California Achievement Tests.

Psychological Corporation
522 Fifth Avenue
New York, New York 10018

Publishers of Academic Promise Tests, Differential Aptitude Tests, Weschler Intelligence Scale for Children, and Mooney Problem Check List. Distributors for Kuhlmann-Anderson Measure of Academic Potential, Rorschach, Henmon-Nelson Tests of Mental Ability, Stanford Achievement Tests, Davis Reading Tests, Gray Oral Reading Tests, Metropolitan Achievement Tests, and Wide Range Vocabulary Test.

Science Research Associates, Inc.
57 West Grand Avenue
Chicago, Illinois 60610

Publishers of SRA Primary Mental Abilities, Iowa Every-Pupil Tests, Test of Educational Ability, and SRA Junior Inventory.

Teachers College Press
Teachers College
Columbia University
New York, N. Y.

Publishers of Gates-MacGinitie Survey Reading Tests, and Durkin-Meshover Phonics Knowledge Survey.

World Book Company
Yonkers-on-Hudson, New York 10005

Publishers of Otis Quick-Scoring Mental Ability Tests, Durrell-Sullivan Reading Capacity and Achievement Tests, and Stanford Achievement Tests.

Houghton Mifflin Company
53 West 43rd Street
New York, New York

Publishers of Lorge-Thorndike Intelligence Tests, and Iowa Every-Pupil Tests of Basic Skills.

Cooperative Test Division
Educational Testing Service
Princeton, New Jersey

Publishers of School and College Ability Tests, and Sequential Tests of Educational Progress.

American Guidance Services Inc.
Circle Pines, Minn. 55014

Western Psychological Services
Div. of Manson Western Corp.
12031 Wilshire Blvd.
Los Angeles, Calif. 90025

Index